BUILD IT LIKE BENJYFISHY AND MRSAVAGE:

THE UNOFFICIAL FORTNITE ESPORTS GUIDE FOR PLAYERS AND PARENTS

CONTENTS

Johnny at his desk working on his blog www.deeperdown.com. Photo credit Frang Foto.

Anne and Benjy at Anne's desk. Photo credit Emily Mudie Photography.

Martin at a photoshoot for his 'No signal' hoodie. Photo credit Trygve Espejord.

INTRODUCTION

Becoming a professional Fortnite player is not just about having talent. There are many aspects to consider when building a career in esports – as the mother of Benjy "benjyfishy" Fish and father of Martin "MrSavage" Foss Andersen we have learned this the hard way. We started our journey into the world of esports when our sons signed with the esports organisation NRG. As parents of professional players, we both faced similar challenges, as we soon discovered there was not the same kind of guidance and information about the esports industry as there is for traditional sports and athletes. We became supportive friends, helping each other navigate the logistical feats of signing contracts with esports organisations, and providing all the administrative and technical support it takes to manage a player and their business. We have travelled the world supporting our sons who have trained at bootcamps and competed in Fortnite tournaments, most notably the Fortnite World Cup 2019 in New York.

In this book, we share our experience and key advice for players and their parents. We also explain how we helped Benjy and Martin manage the difficult challenges that come with being a professional player: from creating a balance between gaming and education, to dealing with tournament disappointments and social media negativity. The book provides a comprehensive guide to building a successful career as a professional Fortnite player, as well as offering a unique insight into esports as a whole, featuring exclusive interviews with leading figures in the industry. It explores how education institutions around the world are incorporating esports into their curriculum, and what career pathways are also open to players.

This book may not teach you about Fortnite gameplay or tactics, but if you want to build your career like tournament champions Benjy and Martin, or you are a parent looking for guidance for your child, you have found the right book.

We also hope that teachers, coaches, family members and other important adults for young gamers will find this book interesting and useful.

Anne Fish and Johnny Troset Andersen

ESPORTS ORGANISATIONS

Esports organisations are management companies who scout talented players to sign, across multiple games, including Fortnite.

For aspiring professional gamers hoping to turn their passion for gaming into a full-time career, joining a top-tier organisation is the starting point of becoming a professional esports player.

THIEVES
APP
OUND

Members of 100 Thieves outside their esports team facility, the Cash App Compound in Los Angeles, USA. From left to right: Brooke "BrookeAB" Ashley Bond, Joseph "Mako" Kelsey, Matthew "Nadeshot" Haag (CEO), Erind "Froste" Puka, Jack "CouRage" Dunlop, Yan "Classify" Shalamov, Rachell "Valkyrae" Hofstetter, Brandon "Avalanche" Thomas, Mohammad "Yassuo" Abdalrhman. Photo credit 100 Thieves.

ESPORTS ORGANISATIONS

An esports organisation (sometimes called a team or clan) signs players to compete in competitive video games and represent them in tournaments.

For a player to sign with a top esports organisation is the equivalent of a traditional sports person being signed by a Premier League football team like Liverpool or Manchester United, or signing for an NFL team, such as Kansas City Chiefs or Seattle Seahawks.

Just as there are different football or NFL divisions similarly there are different tiers of esports organisations. Smaller organisations might not be able to offer as much support to a player or a stable salary, compared to some of the top organisations.

TRAINING FOR ESPORTS

There is a general misconception that professional players do not need to physically train, as esports is classified as a 'mind sport', although in countries such as USA and South Korea they are recognised as professional athletes.

To be a professional esports player requires hours of training, both mentally, in order to develop

SEVERAL TOP FOOTBALL PLAYERS HAVE NOW INVESTED AND STARTED ESPORTS ORGANISATIONS INCLUDING:

DAVID BECKHAM
Guild

SEAD KOLASINAC
Gamma Gaming

MESUT ÖZIL
M10

techniques and skills, as well as physically, to improve reaction time and hand-eye coordination.

Sustaining a healthy and balanced mental and physical regime is crucial to becoming a successful professional esports player. Both Benjy and Martin work out and maintain a healthy diet; Benjy goes to a gym while Martin works out at home. The boys make the extra effort to remain mentally and physically agile, as there is always pressure to maintain a high standard and win tournaments, with new skilled players bidding for the top spot.

GETTING SIGNED

Getting signed with an esports organisation is a key first step for aspiring professional players to realise their dream. However, you do not need to be signed with an organisation to play and compete in Fortnite. The tournaments are open to everyone to compete in and are a great way to get noticed.

Most professional Fortnite players will opt to play on a personal computer (PC) rather than a console. This is because a PC is more versatile, displaying higher refresh rates and having more keys, allowing players to become more proficient in the game. It is important for players to place high in the various weekly cash cup tournaments and Fortnite Champion Series (FNCS) as this is the first crucial step to getting noticed by an organisation. Organisations offer numerous benefits and support including a behind-the-scenes team that can help with a player's growth within the esports space.

When an organisation offers a player a contract, it is important to get professional advice from others. A specialised esports lawyer will check over contracts and offer legal advice on the length of contract and termination clauses. Additionally, the job of an esports agent is to represent a player, and liaise with organisations and sponsors on their behalf, to get the best deal. A lawyer or an agent will help research different organisations to establish if they meet the individual needs and values of a player.

If you receive an offer from an organisation, be sure to consider the following factors:

Seek legal advice on your contract. **1**

Research the organisation. **2**

Find an agent (remember to inquire about their monthly commission). **3**

Find out what the monthly remuneration is and what percentage of any prize money will be deducted. **4**

Find out if there is a monthly streaming requirement or extra social media commitments. **5**

Martin posing with his trophy at 100 Thieves' Cash App Compound after winning DreamHack Anaheim 2020. Photo credit 100 Thieves.

Benjy and Martin playing Fortnite duos at Benjy's home in May 2019. Photo credit MrSavage.

BENJY JOINS NRG ESPORTS

Anne: 'Benjy became duo partners with Martin in February 2019. After only a short while of duoing together, they proved their prowess when they won the SCRIMcom EU Pro Clash Tournament. Then, only three days later, the boys played as a duo in a MontanaBlack Tournament, which they won and received the first prize of $20k between them.

Around the same time, Epic Games decided to lower the age restrictions for the Fortnite World Cup. Previously, players had to be sixteen years old at minimum to compete but now this had been lowered to thirteen years old, meaning that Benjy and Martin (both aged fourteen at the time) could play. Their recent wins, combined with the age restriction announcement, resulted in several esports organisations getting in contact with us. After weighing up the options and offers from different organisations, it felt the right choice for Benjy to join Martin (who was already signed) at NRG. On 19th March 2019 Benjy announced on his evening stream that he had signed with them.'

Left to right, front row: Ben "Edgey" Peterson, Cody "Clix" Conrod, Benjy, "Ronaldo". Back row: Shane " EpikWhale" Cotton, Williams "Zayt" Aubin, Dominick "Unknown Army" Green . Photo credit NRG.

NRG FACTS

 Mark Mastrov and Andy Miller (who co-own the NBA Basketball team, The Sacramento Kings) founded NRG in 2015.

 NRG is based in Los Angeles, California.

 NRG competes in several games including Rocket League, Valorant and Apex Legends.

 NRG's Fortnite roster includes Clix, Ronaldo, EpikWhale, Unknown Army, Edgey and Zayt.

 The San Francisco Shock is NRG's Overwatch League team and were the champions in the 2019 and 2020 seasons.

 Famous NRG investors include Shaquille O'Neal, Jennifer Lopez and Ryan Howard.

 In November 2020, NRG launched the world's first gaming content castle, in downtown Los Angeles.

❝ So happy to have you (Benjy) in the #nrgfam. NRG Fortnite roster is scary now! Boys gonna do some damage. ❞

Andy Miller, NRG Founder and CEO

Photo credit MrSavage.

> **My dream ever since I was a kid was to be a pro gamer, literally I always just played games just so I could try and become pro and this year has been easily the best year of my life.**
>
> *Benjy*

Benjy and Martin at Martin's home in April 2019.
Photo credit MrSavage.

MARTIN JOINS 100 THIEVES

Johnny: 'In February 2020, Martin, Peter (Martin's manager) and I arrived in Los Angeles, five days before the DreamHack Anaheim Tournament. Our early arrival allowed time for Martin to practise and get rid of any jetlag, as we had a secret mission!

It was not yet public knowledge that Martin had just signed with the esports organisation 100 Thieves and we needed time to prepare for the announcement, which was scheduled to happen the day before the tournament.

By that time, Martin had been with NRG for just over a year. He had a lot of friends there including his duo partner Benjy. Therefore the decision to leave was not an easy one. It was the result of a culmination of a couple of months' work for us, as we were weighing up the pros and cons. Leaving an organisation doesn't mean that a player has to lose their teammates and friends. Martin is still good friends with the players and managers at NRG and Benjy and Martin have continued to play together.

There were a lot of factors involved in Martin's decision to sign with 100 Thieves. The facilities at their headquarters, which offered areas for training, streaming, content production and apparel design, played a very important part in his decision. In the end, 100 Thieves felt closer to Martin's heart, and with all financial considerations met, this sealed the deal and Martin signed up.'

Martin photographed meeting Nadeshot (Founder and CEO) on his first day at 100 Thieves. Photo credit 100 Thieves.

Johnny: 'During the week we were in Los Angeles, Peter supervised all the 100 Thieves publicity activities. Peter liaised with 100 Thieves on Martin's behalf and made sure everything was in line with the MrSavage brand. He also made sure Martin attended all the events including the photo-shoots, filming, social media and sponsor appointments. He made sure to minimise any distractions that could disrupt Martin's primary focus which was on playing in the tournament.

While Peter was overseeing the events, I took on the role as the driver as well as taking care of the behind-the-scenes jobs, like grocery shopping and making meals. All in all, it was a lot of work and late hours and both Peter and I were quite exhausted upon returning home.'

> **One of the reasons why I decided to join 100 Thieves is because it looks like a big old family. Being in the Cash App Compound is really nice as well. It also allows me to practise in NA. NA practice is way better than EU practice.**
>
> *Martin*

> **Welcome MrSavage to 100 Thieves!**
>
> **MrSavage qualified 4x for the 2019 Fortnite World Cup and placed T30 in both Solos & Duos. This 15-year-old Norwegian phenom has solidified his spot as a top competitor and creator in the scene. We're beyond excited to have him on 100 Thieves!**
>
> **100 Thieves,** *February 2020*

100 THIEVES FACTS

100 Thieves are a premium lifestyle brand and gaming organisation based in Los Angeles, California.

Matthew "Nadeshot" Haag, a former professional Call of Duty player, founded 100 Thieves in 2017.

100 Thieves compete in games like League of Legends, Valorant and Fortnite.

Over fifty influencers and gamers on their roster include CouRage, BrookeAB and Hiko.

Well-known investors include Drake, Scooter Braun and Sequoia.

100 Thieves' mission is to give every gamer something to be proud of.

> **I'm really looking forward to continue creating content and streaming but the main thing I'm here to do is to win!**
>
> *Martin*

Martin at his first day as a member of 100 Thieves. Photo credit 100 Thieves.

INTERVIEW WITH
ANDY MILLER
Founder and CEO of NRG Esports

Andy is a businessman and entrepreneur within technology, sports and esports. He is a co-owner of the Sacramento Kings of the National Basketball Association (NBA). In 2015 he founded NRG where he works as a CEO.

HOW DID YOU GET INTERESTED IN ESPORTS?

Andy: 'My teen boys were way into gaming and watching Twitch. I started to watch with them back in 2015 and was blown away by the viewer numbers and fan engagement.'

WHY DID YOU DECIDE TO START UP NRG?

Andy: 'I showed my fellow Kings owners various player Twitch streams and dug into the numbers. Mark Mastrov (Kings co-owner and founder of 24 Hour Fitness chain) and I decided to partner up and jump into esports. We bought a League of Legends team in 2016 and soon after Shaquille O'Neal joined the founding group.'

HOW DID YOU COME UP WITH THE NAME NRG? WHICH WE KNOW IS TO BE PRONOUNCED ENERGY AS OPPOSED TO THE LETTERS N.R.G!

Andy: 'It DOES stand for eNeRGy, but most casters still say N.R.G after all these years! The name developed after watching a long time League of Legends Korean player retire and give his final interview after the World Championships. He talked about how he would always remember the feeling of the fans giving him their energy and how special it was to have people rooting for you to do well in life. I loved the positive message behind it and used the letters to abbreviate energy.'

WHAT ARE THE BEST PARTS OF RUNNING AN ESPORTS ORGANISATION?

Andy: 'I love working with the players and watching them grow with the org and grow their own brands. Not everyone becomes a 'Benjy' in terms of fanbase, but we do try to help them mature, take responsibility for themselves, learn what it is like to be part of a team and share common goals etc. Watching them blow up or watching a team get to the top and stay there like our back-to-back World Championship Overwatch team (San Francisco Shock) is super gratifying.'

HOW DO YOU THINK ESPORTS ORGANISATIONS WILL DEVELOP DURING THE NEXT YEARS?

Andy: 'I think the key to successful orgs with staying power will be a dual focus on competitive and content. The content game needs to become a much bigger part of every org's game plan to drive fandom and revenue. I also see a handful of truly global orgs developing that will compete at the highest levels for fans and championships on a regional level as well as a global level.'

Photo credit Andy Miller.

NRG HAS QUITE A LARGE FORTNITE ROSTER WHO PLAY IN LIVE COMPETITIONS. WHAT IS YOUR TAKE ON THE FUTURE OF COMPETITIVE FORTNITE?

Andy: 'I think the COVID-19 pandemic really impacted Fortnite significantly. Maybe the most significantly of all the esports. Fortnite is truly a global, social game and needs to have live global competition and events and celebrations of the game. I think we will see the competitive side of the game become more of a priority for Epic Games in the next couple of years, especially in bringing the community together for live events!'

 NRG HAS A CONTENT CASTLE IN LOS ANGELES, WHERE CREATORS COME TOGETHER ON A PER EVENT BASIS TO MAKE CONTENT. BUT OTHER ORGANISATIONS LIKE FAZE AND 100 THIEVES HAVE CONTENT HOUSES WHERE CREATORS LIVE AND CREATE CONTENT OVER TIME. HOW DO YOU SEE THE FUTURE ON CONTENT CASTLES VS CONTENT HOUSES?

Andy: 'NRG has had content houses over the years. They never last long! Players eventually get tired of them or want their own space and privacy over a period of time. The Castle was a brilliant idea developed by NRG Executive Producer Grady Rains. We wanted a cool, clubhouse type of place that both the players AND the fans would want to be a part of. We make loads of content in the Castle, the Shock scrims and plays from the practice rooms and our staff loves to hang out there. We will continue to do short-term, cool location team-specific houses like we have done for Fortnite in the past.'

 WHY IS IT IMPORTANT FOR YOU TO INVOLVE THE PARENTS AND FAMILY IN THE EARLY TALKS WITH YOUNG PROSPECTIVE PLAYERS WHO YOU WANT TO SIGN?

Andy: 'I am involved in all player talks. Every one! Our motto has always been #NRGFAM and it is with meaning and purpose. Our players came up with the hashtag early on because we all are super involved in everyone who works with the org. It is especially important when signing young players like Benjy and Martin to get to know the families and understand their goals and limitations for their kids. We always sign a player with the intention that they will be with NRG for as long as they want to be. So we want to make sure we really know the player and not just their stream persona.'

 WHAT KIND OF FORTNITE TALENT ARE YOU LOOKING FOR IN THE FUTURE?

Andy: 'NRG has had the top competitive and most popular team for a while now. It is rare to have such talented players who are also fabulous entertainers and trend setters. That is the lens through which we look for Fortnite players. A combo of skill and content creation/stream appeal.'

 FINALLY, ANY ADVICE FOR YOUNG ASPIRING PROFESSIONAL PLAYERS?

Andy: 'Work on your game. Learn to communicate with your fellow players. Be a leader AND a good listener. Understand that the competitive side is a business so building your brand and helping the org build their brand simultaneously gives the org value for the contract. Remember to have fun while playing. If the actual competitive part doesn't bring you joy, then it is not for you.'

JACOB TOFT-ANDERSEN

VP Esports at 100 Thieves

Jacob had a nine-year career as a Dota 2 professional player prior to becoming VP Esports at 100 Thieves in 2019. Jacob also held similar senior positions at Infinite Esports & Entertainment, North Esports and FC Schalke 04, as well as working as a coach, analyst and commentator. Before Martin signed with 100 Thieves, Jacob made the special effort to fly to Oslo, Norway to meet him and his family.

 WHY DID YOU BECOME A PROFESSIONAL PLAYER?

Jacob: 'At the age of eighteen I was playing a lot of video games due to a car accident I had been in which kept me indoors. I had been playing sports competitively my entire life, so it was nice to have something I could devote myself to while recovering. I was always very driven, wanting to be the best, and it didn't take long for teams and companies to reach out.'

 DID YOU GET ANY SUPPORT FROM YOUR PARENTS?

Jacob: 'In my teen years, my dad would drive me to LAN centres for me to play with my friends, and my parents would give me video games for birthdays. But my mom, in particular, struggled with accepting my pro-career. It was frowned upon, in part, because of how big of a toll it took on my attention to my education.'

 COULD YOU ELABORATE ON YOUR ROLE AND RESPONSIBILITIES AT 100 THIEVES?

Jacob: 'My focus is on which titles we are competing in. I ensure that the priorities of the company at large are in line with the esports department; the hiring, scouting and analysis of staff and players, our relationship with the leagues, developers, external teams and players.'

 COACHES PLAY AN IMPORTANT PART IN ESPORTS, EXCEPT PERHAPS FORTNITE. WHY IS THAT AND HOW DO YOU THINK THIS WILL DEVELOP?

Jacob: 'There is a lack of structured events that would encourage more professional frameworks and player improvement. Coaches are predominantly used for more team-heavy titles that run five man line-ups, rather than games that have a lot of individual performance. The game itself appeals to a much younger audience than its competitors, which could be a reason why there is less of a serious approach to the competitive side.'

 IS IT NECESSARY FOR PROFESSIONAL PLAYERS TO HAVE A SOCIAL MEDIA PRESENCE?

Jacob: 'It often depends on the game. Organisations are often happy to compromise with a player's social media presence in order to get the best available talent, but for a lot of organisations it is naturally a very welcomed addition in estimating the overall value of a player. In general, it isn't really all that important to maintain your social media channels (minus YouTube/Twitch), and there are plenty of examples of some of the most popular players in the world who rarely ever use their social media platforms, yet they attract massive attention and crowds of fans.'

Q **SO, YOU ARE SAYING THAT YOUTUBE AND TWITCH ARE IMPORTANT? COULD YOU EXPLAIN WHY AND DOES THE IMPORTANCE DIFFER FROM AN ORGANISATION PERSPECTIVE VERSUS A PLAYER PERSPECTIVE?**

Jacob: 'They are, if the player is focused on growing an audience and an additional revenue stream for themself, not only in the now and immediate future but also as a safety net for if and when their career as a competitor comes to an end. For the organisation, it's metrics added to the size of their following/fanbase. Besides serving as an additional revenue stream as well, depending on whether they get a share via the player's contract, those numbers are often used in sponsorship and partnership pitches and give the teams additional leverage outside of their own team-specific channels.'

Q **HOW DO YOU THINK ESPORTS ORGANISATIONS WILL DEVELOP DURING THE NEXT YEARS?**

Jacob: 'Organisations need to diversify their businesses. Esports lacks the substantial venue entry sales made by traditional sports, they also have smaller merchandise revenues, and licensing rights fees. Everything from sponsorship sales, content creation and additional business opportunities are focal points of staying afloat until esports hits a breakeven point. The organisations will need to continue increasing in size, expertise and manpower to keep up with industry developments.'

Photo credit 100 Thieves.

From left to right: Kyle "Mongraal" Jackson, Victor and Benjy. Photo credit Victor Bengtsson.

VICTOR BENGTSSON

Former talent manager at Fnatic

In 2018, Victor Bengtsson relocated from Sweden to work as a talent manager for the esports organisation Fnatic in London, UK. We spoke to Victor back in February 2021 about his role at Fnatic and what he looks for in new talent, specifically within Fortnite. Victor has since left Fnatic and moved on to talent management for the hugely popular British YouTube group 'Sidemen'.

Q COULD YOU TELL US A LITTLE BIT ABOUT YOUR BACKGROUND?

Victor: 'It all started with a video game, for me it was Mafia, then it was Unlimited Saga and then Morrowind. Eventually my interest turned to more competitive titles such as Call of Duty. As I got older, I decided to study Strategic Communication and Political Science. The idea was to work as a campaign manager with politicians. What I ended up doing isn't that much different. I worked in the Swedish start-up community, eventually I scored a great gig at Volvo where I worked in their creative department for a while. From there, well Fortnite was released and my life took a very different turn.'

Q WHAT DOES YOUR ROLE AS A TALENT MANAGER CONSIST OF?

Victor: 'The day to day is very different depending on the projects we are currently working on. I sit within the talent department, which works towards creating the best possible esports and gaming platform for talent across the world. Someone who is great at playing video games does not necessarily know what is great for them in the world of business, social media and life outside the screen. This is where I come in.'

Q WHAT ESPORTS GAMES ARE YOU MAINLY LOOKING AT?

Victor: 'Fnatic is a multi-title organisation that focuses on titles of relevance across the world. My background has been within the Battle Royale genre and is what I work primarily with.'

Q WHAT ARE YOU LOOKING FOR WHEN SIGNING A PLAYER?

Victor: 'For me, politeness, hard work and ambition often stand out. There are several other factors that are important such as skill level, previous experience and performance in recent tournaments. The key thing however, is the feeling of this person could be great, great beyond his or her title. It is hard to put a finger on it but when you experience it and find it – it is almost magical.'

Q HOW DO YOU SCOUT FOR TALENT?

Victor: 'It is a process of understanding a community and a scene. A lot of hours going into actually reviewing competitive achievements through streams, VODs and clips. At other times, it is understanding who a player is through their positioning on social media and if they fit the vision that your team has. Scouting is one of the most important parts of building a competitive roster.'

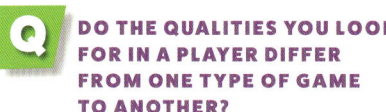

DO THE QUALITIES YOU LOOK FOR IN A PLAYER DIFFER FROM ONE TYPE OF GAME TO ANOTHER?

Victor: 'There are different expectations depending on the age of the player. You cannot expect a 15-year-old to know as much about the world as a 25-year-old. They will make mistakes and that is fine. When you look for whatever greatness is, it translates across games. There is a spark in their eyes, a way they approach their grind, a sense of love for the dream.'

WHAT KIND OF FORTNITE PLAYERS DO YOU LOOK FOR?

Victor: 'Seeing a talent across his or her socials, stream and competitive performance is the base level. Additionally, you have things like understanding the value of listening to people who try to help you, respecting your body and mind and never doubting that it is possible. Not everyone makes it, but you need to fully dedicate yourself to the idea that you will be the one who does.'

FORTNITE IS A GAME THAT CHANGES FROM SEASON TO SEASON, DOES THIS AFFECT THE TYPE OF PLAYERS YOU LOOK FOR?

Victor: 'Even if the changes in Fortnite are way bigger than in other titles, they are still just changes. A player who can adjust will always do better than someone who can't.'

WHEN YOU SIGN A PLAYER DO YOU INVOLVE THE PARENTS FOR YOUNG PLAYERS AND, IF SO, HOW?

Victor: 'Security for minors on the Internet is super important. If a player is underage, we always contact the parents if there is an interest. Negotiations, contracts, conversations and visits to the Fnatic HQ are always facilitated with the parent(s).'

HOW DO YOU FOLLOW UP WITH YOUNG PLAYERS, AFTER HAVING SIGNED THEM. DO YOU TRAVEL TO TOURNAMENTS WITH THEM?

Victor: 'This depends on the title, as there are different age limits for different games. Due to these restrictions, different tournaments require different preparations. For us, it is about creating a professional, comfortable and safe experience if it is a LAN or bootcamp. So, if there is an underage player, the coach and the manager would always be present. If you take major tournaments, the parents are always involved in the travels.'

ARE THERE ANYTHING ASPIRING PLAYERS SHOULD AVOID DOING?

Victor: 'Don't like things on Twitter that come across as unprofessional (everyone who follows you sees this). Don't think that playing the game well is enough. Don't be late to meetings. Don't treat your dream like a hobby – treat it like a career option.

Don't neglect the fact that there's so much more to learn while you're chasing your dream. Fortnite is the only thing you know, learn everything else.'

Q WHAT SHOULD AN ASPIRING PROFESSIONAL PLAYER DO TO GET NOTICED?

Victor: 'Showcase your talent. Be hard working. Be better than yesterday. Do not have different names on different platforms. Treat the players above you with respect. Without connection and friendship, you will either sit alone at the bottom or unliked at the top. Becoming a pro is rare and becoming a pro in a video game is very rare. Share that journey with people you trust and like. When I hear great things about an up-and-coming player outside of the game, that instantly gets my attention. Joining an org doesn't mean you're done — it means you're good enough to begin.'

23

SUPPORT TEAM

Benjy and Martin became professional players in a very short space of time with little knowledge about the esports industry; they had to learn fast and so did the people around them.

The attention from general media outlets, sponsors and fans continues to grow in a professional player's career. The amount of work involved can often be too much for one person to manage therefore a support team is a key requirement.

PARENT SUPPORT

The age range of players who start their professional Fortnite playing career is between thirteen and eighteen, with the majority being at the younger end of the scale. At that age players will probably not have a basic understanding of business and life skills, so it is important for parents, and a player's extended family and friends, to be able to guide and support them.

Johnny: 'As a parent, we advise you to learn a little about Fortnite, follow what tournaments are taking place, and if there are any LAN tournaments happening. This will give you a better understanding as to how to support your child. Whilst teenagers can be challenging at times try to work as a team with them on a common goal.

If players start earning money consistently, whether that is from placement in tournaments, streaming revenue, or YouTube, players in effect become self-employed and are running a business. There are requirements that come with that, for example getting accounts prepared, organising bank accounts, paying taxes, setting up a company (depending on individual circumstances) and taking legal advice on contracts if they are approached by an organisation or sponsors.

It is important to get professional advice from accountants and lawyers who have an understanding of esports, influencers and content creators, as there can be some unique challenges. For example with tax, there are different tax systems in different countries, therefore you should seek more specialist advice in the country you are based.'

Anne: 'Benjy joined NRG in March 2019 after Martin had already signed for them in January of the same year. Shortly after this, Benjy and I went to Oslo in Norway to meet Martin and his family. It was very useful for us to be able to talk and share experiences about navigating the world of esports and professional gaming.

Admittedly, when I left Oslo, I felt even more overwhelmed by what Johnny had to say, than when I had arrived. There is so much that goes on behind the scenes of managing a professional player, but it was good to know that Benjy and I were not alone. It is one of the reasons why both Johnny and I want to help and advise parents who are new to esports as well as future esports professional players.'

MANAGERS

If the support tasks become too many, consider hiring a manager to help.

Johnny: 'Initially I started out as Martin's manager, but after just a few months we hired Peter Rudi Pettersen (see interview with Peter at page 30) to help out part-time, which later evolved to a full-time position. I am still greatly involved in Martin's team but more on the technical, legal and overall business side of things, while Peter handles day-to-day scheduling and activities with the esports organisation, social media, sponsorships, his agency and general media.'

Martin: 'Having Peter as my personal manager saves me a lot of time and allows me to focus on what matters most to me, namely practice and tournaments. Peter acts as my single point of contact towards almost everything that goes on – and it is a lot! Peter is simply invaluable and I'm so glad that we have him on our core team.'

Anne: 'I act as Benjy's manager with help from his organisation and his agency in all the logistical and practical aspects of his career. I arrange all travel, accommodation and tournament schedules as well as external negotiations and legal matters.'

Johnny: 'Since 2019 the workload to manage Martin's business has increased. Therefore in 2020 we hired Teodor Thoresen Skarpaas to help Peter out with social media tasks.'

LAWYERS

Before any contract is signed, it is in the best interest of players to consult with an esports lawyer. They can help, for example, to negotiate an esports organisation agreement on your behalf as well as checking out sponsorship contracts and assisting with any copyright issues and more.

Anne and Johnny at the players' lounge during the 2019 Fortnite World Cup finals in New York City. Photo credit MrSavage.

ACCOUNTANTS

Benjy and Martin both have a Limited Liability Company (LLC) set up to protect their interests. Having an esports accountant who understands the intricacies of the different revenue streams, including how tax works with Epic Games' prize money and the regulations within your specific country, is essential.

TECH ADVISERS

Even though Benjy and Martin know a lot about Fortnite settings, they are not experts at configuring their PCs and hardware for their gameplay and streaming. Early in their career they relied on friends and family to help out with the technical side of gaming.

Anne: 'Benjy's older brother Charles initially helped out with his PC set-up. Later Benjy chose to use Luke Davies from CLD Computers, a local computer shop, to assist him.'

Johnny: 'I still take care of the tech support for Martin, but I lean heavily on Roberth "Fantonald" Hansen, a local PC and hardware specialist and Marc Serra, an IT infrastructure specialist out of Barcelona, Spain. Roberth's young son Daniel "Cobra" Hansen does all the initial testing of Martin's new PCs, making sure Fortnite always behaves as smoothly as possible.'

INFLUENCER AGENCIES

Managing the demands of the esports industry can be hard, even with the help of managers, lawyers and an organisation.

As in traditional sports, an agent is someone who looks after a player or other talent's best interests, whether that is securing sponsorship deals, handling their image or negotiating better organisation agreements for them.

An agent will represent a player, caster or other esports professional. They will aim to do whatever is in their clients' best interests and will usually take a commission on deals and contracts secured.

Some agencies may also act as advisors, or personal assistants to their clients, managing their schedules, such as booking accommodation and travel for promotional activities. Others will handle a brand or individual's image or arrange commercial partnerships on their behalf.

Johnny: 'After the Fortnite World Cup in 2019 I realised that more help was needed for managing Martin's career. After reviewing offers from several agencies, Cengiz Tüylü, the founder and former CEO of Germany's most successful esports team 'mousesports', was hired and has proved a very close and valuable partner ever since. I'm proud to say that Cengiz has become a good friend of mine.'

Martin: 'Cengiz seems to know everyone within esports, having been involved in esports since the early 2000s. I mean, with his team he won several world championships in different games! Being able to tap into his experience is simply amazing.'

Anne: 'There was a lot of interest from agencies to sign Benjy but after careful consideration we chose to sign up with Loaded in January 2021.'

Benjy: 'I was approached by several agencies looking to represent me but decided that Loaded was the best fit for my brand and aligned with my goals for the future.'

The Coalition of Parents in Esports (COPE) offers mentoring and advice to parents, in addition to a wealth of information about esports (see COPE chapter, page 218).

ORGANISATION SUPPORT

Some esports organisations can assist with a variety of services including:

COACHING

BOOTCAMPS

VIDEO EDITORS

PERIPHERALS

SPONSORSHIP OPPORTUNITIES

TRAVEL TO LAN TOURNAMENTS

COMPUTER SETUP

GRAPHIC DESIGNERS

CONTENT CREATION

Cengiz (right) together with Ola "Element" Moum at ESL Katowice Major 2019. Ola is a Norwegian Counter-Strike Legend, member of the Esports Hall of Fame and a good friend of both Peter and Cengiz. Photo credit Cengiz Tüylü.

Photo credit Erik Hem, Twins Productions.

PETER RUDI PETTERSEN

Martin's Personal Manager and Player Manager for 100 Thieves

We have asked Peter to shed some light about his role.

HOW DID YOU BECOME MARTIN'S MANAGER?

Peter: 'In late 2018, I watched videos of a crazy talented fourteen-year-old placing second in the Fortnite Winter Royale EU Qualifiers. To my great surprise, I found that he lived only ten minutes away! I decided to go for it, prepared myself well, got a meeting with Johnny and presented my views on how to develop Martin's brand. I started part-time focusing on the social media side, but it gradually evolved to a full-time position as a manager as his popularity grew.'

HOW MUCH IS MARTIN INVOLVED ON SOCIAL MEDIA?

Peter: 'Initially Martin did everything, but shortly after signing NRG in early 2019 it became clear that it was impossible for him to cope with the explosion of followers and the increasing demand for content. Nowadays, Martin approves posts, clips and videos that differ in style from previous material and he does all Tweets himself. He spends around half an hour each day overseeing his social media, including reading and liking comments, plus providing feedback to me.'

WHAT ARE YOUR MAIN RESPONSIBILITIES?

Peter: 'I'm the single point-of-contact for every request going to or from Martin and coordinate all his activities with 100 Thieves, sponsors, vendors, and the general media. I'm also in charge of his social media, but day-to-day video and clip editing and posting are done by an almost full-time employed Channel Manager (Teodor "Th0rn3d" Thoresen Skarpaas). Teodor handles contracted video and graphics editors and stream moderators and takes on some of the video editing himself. I report to Johnny, who handles legal matters, accounting and all of Martin's business operations.'

WHAT IS MOST IMPORTANT IN YOUR ROLE?

Peter: 'Definitely to make room for Martin as a talent to develop in the direction he wants – which is mainly competitive – and support him by alleviating any obstacles in his path. This means to really pay attention to his needs, to help him adjust his direction and say yes to only the most fitting requests from sponsors and media. I also have a responsibility to tell him when I disagree. This is something that is important for Martin's family, as they don't want to risk Martin burned out at a young age by saying yes too much. However, it is very clear that in the end all decisions are Martin's. Martin is the boss!'

Martin and Peter in New York City during the 2019 World Cup co-ordinating activities. Photo credit MrSavage.

DOES EVERY PROFESSIONAL PLAYER NEED A PERSONAL MANAGER?

Peter: 'Martin didn't at the start of his career, and I worked part-time until he passed about 1 million followers across his social media. However, Johnny did a lot of manager tasks the first months before shifting to a more business oversight role. I guess a parent, a relative or a friend can act part-time as a manager for a period, until the amount of work becomes overwhelming. It also helps to join an organisation and get help from the organisation's player manager. All in all, I guess it is a question of timing that depends on the player's popularity, but also ambitions, as a full-time manager most likely will accelerate the player's growth and improve his results.'

YOU ARE ALSO A PLAYER MANAGER FOR 100 THIEVES. WHAT DOES THAT INVOLVE?

Peter: 'In the talks leading up to Martin joining 100 Thieves, it became clear that both parties wanted a tight partnership. Making me a 100 Thieves player manager gives me inside information about all relevant things taking place inside the organisation, allowing for a very smooth cooperation both ways. It also allows me to work closely with other players at 100 Thieves to exchange ideas and insights. I have had the joy of working closely with Jackson Dahl (VP Talent and Entertainment), which has been a huge inspiration for me.'

WHAT IS YOUR TOP TIP FOR ASPIRING PROFESSIONAL FORTNITE PLAYERS?

Peter: 'Have fun while you compete! Of course, you need to grind and work hard but remember to take breaks and never forget the fun of competing with friends!'

HOW HAVE YOU ORGANISED THE WORK AROUND CONTENT PRODUCTION?

Peter: 'The main source of content is Martin's streams on Twitch, which are assigned to an editor and a thumbnail designer along with a short description and a checklist of what we want to achieve.

A clip scouter goes through the stream to come up with clip candidates. The resulting video, thumbnail and clips are reviewed by our Channel Manager and me before posting to Martin's various social media channels, which are his three channels on YouTube, his TikTok and stories, reels or IGTV on his Instagram, plus the occasional clips on Twitter.

I shoot most of his photos for regular Instagram posts myself, plus handle other type of content like YouTube vlogs and sponsor posts through contract editors. A single stream can result in multiple videos, clips and posts and involve as much as seven people from start till end(!). We use a Trello board (www.trello.com) to keep track of all steps in these processes.'

FINALLY, DO YOU HAVE ANY ADVICE FOR PARENTS?

Peter: 'I think it is very important for parents to understand that esports and gaming are a very social thing and allow players to share experiences and fun with friends. If you don't understand this, try asking your child to tell you what they do in their games and with friends. If they won't, at least have them share a YouTube video or two that they think explains their hobby — or future career.'

JAIME COHENCA

General Manager and Chief of Staff at NRG Esports

Jaime is Benjy's Player Manager and he has also worked with Martin during his time at NRG. We were interested in hearing more about Jaime's role at NRG but also his experience of working with professional players and their parents.

Q YOU HAVE MULTIPLE ROLES AT NRG. WHAT ARE YOUR RESPONSIBILITIES AND WHAT DOES A NORMAL DAY LOOK LIKE FOR YOU?

Jaime: 'My main role is to oversee recruiting and management of NRG's competitive rosters across all our teams including Fortnite, Valorant, Rocket League, Apex Legends and others, along with non-competitive content creators and talent. I would say almost every day is different for me. Some days are spent on strategy calls, some days recruiting new talent and others planning events or team trips. My role provides a lot of variation in my day to day, which I enjoy!'

Q HOW DID YOU START OUT IN THIS INDUSTRY AND END UP WORKING FOR NRG?

Jaime: 'I grew up playing Counter-Strike competitively, so gaming has always been a huge part of my life. After taking some jobs out of college that I did not really love, I decided I wanted to get involved in esports. I got connected with Brett Lautenbach, NRG's President. I was super excited for the opportunity as I was a fan of their Overwatch team at the time. I began working as an account manager on the partner and sponsorship side, then I transitioned to working with teams and players.'

Q WHAT WAS IT LIKE TO WORK WITH BENJY AND MARTIN?

Jaime: 'I learned a lot from Benjy and Martin, but what I value most is the experience I have gained. It was very new for me to be working with such young, talented people. I realised quickly that they both were much more disciplined and mature when compared to far older players I had worked with. I never once felt like I needed to worry about them posting something distasteful on social media, or that they would lose focus or drive during the season. They are also both extremely humble which is a quality that I admire a lot, so to be able to help them progress and be a part of their path to stardom has been very rewarding for me personally.'

At Dreamhack Anaheim 2020. From left to right: Williams "Zayt" Aubin, Jaime, Ben "Edgey" Peterson, Benjy. Photo credit NRG.

Jaime (left) and Grady Rains. Photo credit NRG.

Jaime handing out gifts to Benjy and Zayt in the lead up to the 2019 Fortnite World Cup in New York City. Photo credit NRG.

At the Fortnite World Cup 2019 in New York City. From left to right: Martin, Benjy, Shane "EpikWhale" Cotton, Jaime, Williams "Zayt" Aubin, Mason "Symfuhny" Lanier. Photo credit NRG.

Q WHAT ARE THE MOST COMMON QUESTIONS PARENTS OF YOUNG NEWLY SIGNED PLAYERS WILL ASK YOU?

Jaime: 'Most parents are interested in making sure their child is in good hands. Many just want to get to know me personally a bit better. Most interactions with parents are just check-ins, making sure their child is doing well. I also get a number of questions around individual sponsorship work from parents, they either need help navigating sponsorship deals, or want advice.'

Q WHAT ARE THE MOST COMMON QUESTIONS FROM NEWLY SIGNED PROFESSIONAL PLAYERS?

Jaime: 'They generally ask questions revolving around social media like "Is it OK to post this?" or "Can I make a custom banner for Twitter?" Most players don't utilise their team's management as much as they should. A lot of my job is helping our players reach their maximum potential, but only a small percentage of players really seek out my help. I would recommend any young player to take advantage of the resources of the org they are signing with. We are here to help you!'

Q HOW IMPORTANT IS THE ROLE PARENTS PLAY IN THE RELATIONSHIP BETWEEN A PROFESSIONAL ESPORTS ORGANISATION AND YOUNG PLAYERS?

Jaime: 'It really depends on the situation. Some parents aren't involved at all in the relationship, while others are very invested. I think parents should focus on working with the org to make sure their child is getting the most value from being with the org as possible.'

Q WHAT ARE YOUR TIPS FOR ASPIRING PROFESSIONAL PLAYERS?

Jaime: 'Set goals and practise with a sense of purpose. Playing mindlessly will never be as effective as constantly focusing on improving. Every match you should be thinking about what you could have done differently and why you are not where you want to be as a player yet. Practice quality over quantity.'

CENGIZ "DJANGO" TÜYLÜ

Martin's agent and advisor

An agent is someone who looks after a player's best interests, including securing sponsorship deals, negotiating with esports organisations and offering career development advice. Cengiz is the co-founder and former CEO of mousesports, one of the most established and successful esports organisations in Germany. In recent years, Cengiz has devoted his time to a select group of talented players including Martin.

 **HOW DID YOU BECOME MARTIN'S AGENT AND ADVISOR?**

Cengiz: 'Martin's manager Peter is a good friend and protégé of the Norwegian Counter-Strike Legend, Ola "Element" Moum. Ola played for mousesports back in 2011, and I met him again a few years later, when he was inducted in the Esports Hall of Fame. In early 2019, Ola told me about Peter, who managed a talented Fortnite kid called MrSavage, whose parents were actively looking for representation. Ola introduced me to Peter and the Foss Andersen family. The rest is kind of history.'

 **HOW DOES A PLAYER GET REPRESENTATION?**

Cengiz: 'Back in 2015–16, there were no agencies at all. With all the hype and money around esports the later years, a lot of agents have found their way into the industry. A few years ago, players had to look for agents themselves, but nowadays you can expect to get approached at a very early stage of your esports career.'

 **WHAT DO YOU SEE AS THE MOST IMPORTANT ASPECTS OF YOUR JOB?**

Cengiz: 'The commercial aspect is the one people think of at first – like sponsorships and negotiations.

However, I think my most valuable asset is my experience, since I started with esports already in 2002 with mousesports. I have run an esports team and have had the privilege to work with great talent, including Niko "NiKo" Kovac in CSGO, Anton "Cooller" Singov in Quake and Benjamin "Problem X" Simon in Street Fighter, as well as winning championships (such as Counter-Strike World Championship 2008, Quake 4 World Championship 2005 and Street Fighter World Championship 2018), but also playing a role in important and innovative brand partnerships that helped to shape the industry.

I think that is why I'm matching so well with Martin and his team, as we are aiming to help Martin's long-term career doing the right moves.'

Cengiz watching over chrisJ's shoulder during DreamHack Stockholm 2018. Photo credit Cengiz Tüylü.

WHEN SHOULD A PLAYER CONSIDER GETTING AGENT REPRESENTATION?

Cengiz: 'As soon as there is a demand (official offers) from bigger, more established esports organisations. If you don't want to hire an agent, at least have legal counsel for all contracts.'

ARE THERE ANY PITFALLS TO WATCH OUT FOR WHEN HIRING AN AGENCY?

Cengiz: 'I have seen a lot of agents from the traditional sports world entering esports, as they have expansion and growth objectives. However, I think it is very valuable to find experienced people with a heritage within esports, a network within the gaming industry and an understanding of the specific titles. Esports is very different to traditional sports and a still very young entertainment and sports industry.'

DO YOU HANDLE THE LEGAL SIDE AS WELL?

Cengiz: 'I'm in charge of all of Martin's negotiations with brands and esports organisations, but when it comes to detailed contractual work, we are hiring lawyers from all over the world depending on the contract's jurisdiction and content, like employment law or media rights.'

HOW DO AGENCIES GET COMPENSATED?

Cengiz: 'There are certainly several compensation models, but as far as it concerns my work with Martin we agreed on a fixed and monthly percentage commission fee, which is the most common model.'

SHOULD A PLAYER JUST ACCEPT ANY SPONSORSHIP REQUEST?

Cengiz: 'No, of course not. Obviously there needs to be some sort of ethical standard and nobody should accept any sponsorship request per se. Esports professionals are role models for the young generation to come. Personally, I am convinced of a more sustainable and long-term strategy, only working with sponsors that share the same values and offer products that you feel comfortable with using and promoting to your fans. At the same time, decisions are highly influenced through financial factors, so there is a lot to consider on an individual level.'

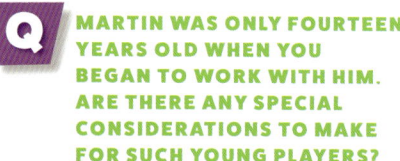

MARTIN WAS ONLY FOURTEEN YEARS OLD WHEN YOU BEGAN TO WORK WITH HIM. ARE THERE ANY SPECIAL CONSIDERATIONS TO MAKE FOR SUCH YOUNG PLAYERS?

Cengiz: 'Getting recognition and fame on social media or even in mainstream media, as in Martin's case, requires a very stable character and realistic perspective on things. It is important not to neglect education, friends and family, as an esports career can end abruptly for reasons beyond one's control, like the game not being popular anymore. It is also very important to have supportive parents with a clear view, conveying the right values and finding the balance between things.

The young player needs to understand that this is work and requires a certain discipline, on the other side it needs to stay fun, because that is the main reason why someone is becoming so good and enthusiastic about playing a video game.'

Cengiz and Martin the day they first met at Martin's home in Oslo, Norway, back in 2019. Photo credit MrSavage.

INTERVIEW WITH

BRANDON FREYTAG

Founder of Loaded, an esports talent management company

Brandon Freytag has worked in esports since the early 2000s. He started out as a CS player as well as a scout, until he went full time as an agent for the esports team Evil Geniuses. Since then he has worked for Twitch, and in 2016 he founded Loaded, the talent management company that works with some of the top esports influencers including Benjy, Shroud, Dakotaz, DrLupo and CouRage.

Q TELL US A BIT ABOUT YOUR BACKGROUND IN ESPORTS.

Brandon: 'After working with many companies selling sponsorships for top gaming teams, tournament organisers and events, I created my own gaming team called Loaded. I saw the opportunity to merge my efforts with Evil Geniuses, where I ended up selling sponsorships for them. I helped contribute to bringing some of the biggest brands at the time into esports, including Monster Energy, T-Mobile and Papa Johns among others. After spinning Evil Geniuses into the parent company GoodGame, we sold the company to Twitch. At Twitch I started to work with more and more influencers helping them grow their business, and advising them based on my prior experience. I saw the opportunity to then leave Twitch and take my adventures full time. I would like to give a special shoutout to Summit1G, Lirik and TimTheTatman for being the first clients of mine and giving me that chance.'

Q YOU HAVE BEEN DESCRIBED AS AN ESPORTS VETERAN – WHAT ARE THE BIGGEST CHANGES YOU HAVE SEEN IN THE INDUSTRY?

Brandon: 'One of the biggest changes that I really pushed for is player and influencer rights when it comes to agreements. Early on, many companies, orgs and other groups took advantage of the lack of knowledge, and saw massive returns from creators. Companies were doing deals for products and players were not getting paid. I felt that dynamic wasn't right and I worked hard to correct that over the years. Fast track to today, the influx of investments and general interest in the space has significantly increased the money for teams, players, influencers and careers in general. When I think back to watching players on CRT monitors wearing shirts with one or two sponsors to where we are now, I wouldn't have guessed it to be this big.'

Q WHAT INSPIRED YOU TO START LOADED?

Brandon: 'I remember asking some creators about their current sponsorships and if they reviewed the agreements they signed. They all said no, so I knew instantly something needed to be done. I knew many of these creators at times were getting more eyeballs than entire esports teams, but were not getting paid nearly enough or even at all! I wanted to fix that! On top of the urgency to correct the space, I genuinely loved watching content creators. Loaded has some pretty basic principles I always try to stick by, which is being honest, trustworthy and simply doing the right thing.'

Q **WHAT ARE THE BEST PARTS OF RUNNING A TALENT MANAGEMENT COMPANY?**

Brandon: 'Having a good relationship with the talent and making their lives easier in some sort of fashion. Increasing a deal, providing advice on a new project, or just being there during a rough time in their lives is very meaningful to me. I treat all of our talent as family here.'

Q **WHAT SERVICES DO LOADED OFFER AND WHAT SETS YOU APART FROM OTHER AGENCIES?**

Brandon: 'We are all gamers at Loaded and are extremely passionate about the success of the space. Unlike other agencies, we solely focus on gaming and because of that we spend all of our resources to grow in this space. Our service level for our talent is top notch; we take great pride in being there for them any time they need something.'

Q **WHAT SKILL SET IS REQUIRED TO BECOME A SUCCESSFUL AGENT?**

Brandon: 'Early on, I watched, I listened, and I worked a ton. You must be a hard worker and be willing to put the hours in. You need to be a great negotiator, especially if you plan to provide value through sales or platform deals as I have done. Everyone is good at something, and you just need to figure out how to tie that back into jump starting your career in this industry.'

Q **WHAT ARE YOUR RESPONSIBILITIES AND WHAT DOES A NORMAL DAY LOOK LIKE FOR YOU?**

Brandon: 'When Loaded was founded I handled everything, but as we have grown our business, I have been able to take on more and more employees. My typical day always starts out with viewing one of our creators in the morning, which I typically leave on and switch throughout the day. I believe it is very important to stay in tuned with each creator, even if it is just a normal stream. After this, I check all the emails, ensure we are moving forward on all our projects and handle any platform deal negotiations I have ongoing until I hit the different meetings I have throughout the day.'

Q **WHAT DO YOU LOOK FOR WHEN SIGNING A CONTENT CREATOR/ INFLUENCER?**

Brandon: 'We understand the entire gaming market and we are watching and taking notes on prospects over time. If we see one we want to pull the trigger on, we have a meeting as a group to get a consensus as a team. It is very important to us that we have all our departments on board before we reach out to offer representation, to ensure we provide the maximum value to each client.'

Q **WHAT WOULD YOUR ADVICE BE TO A PLAYER CONSIDERING GETTING AGENT REPRESENTATION?**

Brandon: 'If you have any income, then you should have some sort of representation. In regard to hiring a full-time manager, I think it really depends on the specific creator. If their business is booming but it is taking away from the content creation side, then maybe it is time to have someone help or handle that, to ensure they can give 100 per cent to content. But there are many creators that can manage both their content and business – and that's OK. But if you are doing any contracts of any kind, you should get a lawyer to review it at the very least.'

Q HOW DID YOU END UP SIGNING BENJY?

Brandon: 'I had an eye on him when the 2019 Fortnite World Cup was happening. I noticed early on he was very gifted at Fortnite and I loved his energy. I reached out and told him that when he felt the time was right, I would love to work with him. Fast track to a few years later, we connected again and made it happen. Benjy knew I would always be there for him when he felt it was the right time to take his career to the next level.'

Q TELL US MORE ABOUT UPDATING BENJY'S BRAND. HOW IMPORTANT DO YOU FEEL THAT THIS IS TO AN INFLUENCER?

Brandon: 'We knew early on that Benjy didn't really have the brand identity needed for his fans to attach even more to him. A brand grows with you and over time that brand potentially lives on without you. The easiest example here is when you think of former professional basketball player Michael Jordan, you don't see his face – you see his iconic Nike Air Jordan logo. Jordan hasn't played for years, but his brand continues to be the most talked about brand for athletes. As Benjy continues to build out his business beyond just his stream, his newly established brand will help carry that forward.'

Q WHAT ARE THE FUTURE PLANS FOR LOADED?

Brandon: 'We are continuing to expand what Loaded does as well as diversify our business. We continuously bring in new employees with different skill sets to help set us apart. We are also going to be getting into more talent-owned projects that we will help facilitate and run, to expand their portfolio as their brands grow. This could include producing unique shows or unique content, as creators are the new entertainers.'

Q WHAT ARE YOUR TOP TIPS FOR PLAYERS TRYING TO BECOME INFLUENCERS?

Brandon: 'Be unique, don't expect to see success right away. Ensure you dedicate the time and be consistent with your schedule, ensure your audience feels connected to you. Ultimately have fun, if you don't enjoy it the audience will know.'

Photo credit Loaded.

BALANCING STUDIES

Balancing studies with a career, as a professional esports player or content creator, is not without its challenges. Both Benjy and Martin have faced difficulties when it comes to combining education with the intense schedule of tournaments and the hours of practice needed to stay at the top.

47

MARTIN AND SCHOOL

Johnny: 'Growing up, Martin attended a private Montessori primary school in Norway. Montessori schools offer an open and curiosity-driven approach to teaching, which suited Martin very well. However, at thirteen Martin changed schools to attend the same local school as his older brother, but he didn't seem to settle into the more traditional classroom style of education. In December 2017, some months after Fortnite was launched, we decided as a family to apply for a place at a new Montessori school for Martin. Fortunately, he was accepted, however his place would not be available until the next school year. In the meantime, we had decided that he should be home schooled which gave him a bit more leisure time for playing football (soccer) and gaming.'

GROWING CHALLENGES

Johnny: 'My wife, Solfrid, and I were completely unaware of Martin's progress in competitive Fortnite until around the time he came second in the online Fortnite Winter Royale EU Qualifiers in November 2018. Things took off rapidly after the Winter Royale and Martin received a handful of offers from top-tier esports organisations around the world. After two months of negotiations Martin ended up choosing NRG in January 2019.'

Fortnite Winter Royale Open Qualifiers 2018

EU TOP SCORES

#1 LeStream Skite
42 [5 Wins] [12 Matches Played]

#2 MrSavage
40 [5 Wins] [9 Matches Played]

#3 FA Ares
40 [4 Wins] [10 Matches Played]

We found the challenge of combining school and competitive esports was increasing at home. Martin was visibly more tired after the long hours of combining full-time schooling with playing Fortnite in the evenings. Both my wife and I had to negotiate with Martin about his bedtime, we also suggested that he should try to spend more time with his friends IRL instead of online. We stressed the importance of maintaining a balance of physical exercise versus sitting in front of the computer.

It was undeniably clear to us that gaming was very important to Martin, and that he had made a community of friends online who he valued very much. We didn't have a recipe for how to handle the situation; we had to learn through discussion and compromise.'

FAMILY AGREEMENT

Johnny: 'The discussions resulted in some informal rules, but as Martin's popularity grew and he signed the contract with NRG, the family needed more formal rules in place.

We set up a family agreement with two pages of various ground rules. Now this may sound strict, but the rules were there first and foremost to discuss and handle expectations from both sides: Martin and his schooling, his gaming and other activities on one side, and the family as a unity on the other side.

We made sure the family agreement stood in line with our values. We had points about purpose (gaming should always be fun), balance (schooling, time off, family life), sleep (minimum eight and a half hours per night) and physical exercise (two days per week). We then implemented these into weekly plans, adjusting when necessary.'

MONTESSORI SCHOOL

Johnny: 'We kept the new Montessori school updated about Martin's advancements within esports and his growing commitments.

It turned out that the school was really flexible with Martin's esports career while still honouring the mandatory requirements, by the quite strict school system in Norway.

Working closely with his school we were able to reduce Martin's hours. This gave him time to practise and participate in both online and LAN tournaments, the latter requiring travelling for as much as two weeks at a time. If he had played in an evening tournament, Martin was often permitted to start his school day later the following morning. During this period, Martin attended school on average about two and a half days per week. He also had sessions prepared for him to attend at home, facilitated by the school's team of teachers, with my wife and I providing additional support.'

FULL-TIME ESPORTS PLAYER

Johnny: 'Martin finished mandatory schooling in June 2020 and we, as a family, decided shortly after that he should take at least one year's leave of absence to become a full-time esports player. Martin has said that he may continue his education later, but at what schools and in which form he didn't know. After all, few teenagers know for sure what future career they want to pursue.

One could say that Martin was partly home schooled during his last Montessori years, but with professional guidance, as it was only made possible through an extraordinary effort by his schoolteachers. Martin, my wife and I will always be grateful for that.'

> " At the start, when I was playing Fortnite, I was home schooled because I was switching schools. There was a six-month period where I was searching for a new school. That was very good timing because I got to grind Fortnite for like half a year. So that kind of boosted me up to one of the top players. "
>
> *Martin*

Martin doing homework. Photo credit MrSavage.

> " Both Benjy and Martin were fourteen years old when the 2018 Fortnite Winter Royale Tournament took place and they were allowed to play the qualifiers but not the finals according to Epic Games' rules at the time. In February 2019 Epic Games changed the rules to allow thirteen-year-olds to compete all the way to the finals. According to the rules for FNCS chapter 2 season 7 (July - October 2021) a player must still meet that age requirement to play any FNCS match. Make sure to check Epic Games' rules and guidelines library before every tournament. "
>
> *Johnny*

BENJY'S EDUCATION

Anne: 'I had always prioritised Benjy's education over everything else. Benjy had attended independent prep schools in Surrey, UK from the ages of three to thirteen. The schools had provided a lot of opportunities for Benjy including encouraging his sporting ambitions.

At thirteen, Benjy took the Common Entrance (CE) exam to progress into his chosen senior school with places highly contested. Benjy would sit exams for the core subjects, Maths, English and the Sciences. Additionally, he sat exams in History, Geography, Religious Studies, French and Spanish. Benjy needed to achieve at least 70 – 80 per cent in each of these assessments if he was to pass. Not only were there exams to sit, but also a pre-test and interview stage of admissions.'

ACING EXAMS

Anne: 'Getting Benjy to do any revision was extremely difficult and involved relentless nagging from my side. After a lot of cajoling, Benjy did manage to put in the necessary revision work, ahead of his CE exam week. I wanted to make sure I was doing all I could to ensure Benjy passed these exams. I firmly believed that when armed with a good education, Benjy would have a strong foundation to build his future, offering him more choices in life.

Even though he didn't particularly like school, and preferred to be gaming, this school was where all his friends were going, and I knew he wouldn't have wanted to miss out. It was a huge relief to finally find out that the work had paid off, and partly due to his natural aptitude and intelligence, Benjy had passed all of his exams.'

BENJY HOME SCHOOLING

Anne: 'The more time Benjy was playing Fortnite, the less time he was spending on his schoolwork. Several tier one esports organisations had contacted Benjy, wanting to sign him, and I knew he couldn't manage a full-time education with a full-time gaming career.

After Benjy qualified for the World Cup in 2019, I tried to work with his school to allow him time to be able to practise and compete at a competitive level. We explored several options including reducing hours to just the core subjects or taking time out from studies. At the time, Benjy's school already offered these options to their golf and tennis academies, who take time out each term to participate in bootcamps and tournaments. The fact that esports tournaments are played late into the evening (especially if Benjy is playing in North American tournaments), often not finishing until the early hours, meant that continuing school was not realistically possible. I then made the difficult decision to home school Benjy and organised tutors to come in to teach lessons.

Home schooling is not going to be a suitable option for everyone, and the decision needs to be considered carefully. However, it can give players the flexibility needed to balance studies with both practice and tournament schedules.'

LIFE'S TOO SHORT... SEIZE THE MOMENT

Anne: 'So many students take a gap year before embarking on either a university course or training scheme but why does it have to be at the age of eighteen? Why not earlier? Life is too short and you ultimately spend all your time working to earn an income. If you have the opportunity to make a career out of something you enjoy then go for it otherwise you will always be wondering what if....'

TOP TIPS

Make your school homework your priority. **1**

Write a schedule of tournaments (with dates and times) and plan your studies around these. **2**

Do not procrastinate and make sure you focus when studying. **3**

Set yourself a daily gaming time-limit and try to stick to it. **4**

Go to bed at a sensible time. **5**

Exercise regularly and try to eat healthily. **6**

Take breaks and have some leisure time when you can relax. **7**

Photo credit benjyfishy.

EDUCATION DOES NOT HAVE AN EXPIRATION DATE

Anne: 'I don't think that education is something fixed or that you have to do exams when you are sixteen or eighteen, as there is nothing stopping you continuing your studies at a later stage. I believe that we continue to have opportunities to learn throughout our lifetime.'

Photo credit NRG.

EDUCATION AND ESPORTS

The education and academic worlds have started to embrace the benefits that esports can offer young people, and recognise that there are transferable skills learnt while gaming, which can help them succeed in future careers.

BENEFITS OF ESPORTS

In 2019 the BBC reported that businesses are waking up to the skills gamers are able to bring to the workplace and there is a growing acceptance that gaming skills are transferable. These skills include:

 TEAMWORK

 LEADERSHIP

 COMMUNICATION

 MULTI-TASKING

 STRATEGIC LEADERSHIP

 ANALYTICAL SKILLS

STRATEGIC THINKING AND ANALYTICAL SKILLS

Being able to analyse and plan your game strategically, as well as being able to re-evaluate in-game when things go wrong, are the key ingredients to achieving the Victory Royale. Both Benjy and Martin have these skills. Martin is known as being one of the best for strategy and analytical skills, earning him the title of "200IQ".

> *The gaming industry is larger than films and music combined, yet few of us are likely to put our Fortnite playing achievements on our CVs. But why not? Businesses are waking up to the skills gamers can bring to the workplace.*
>
> *BBC*

TEAMWORK

Fortnite can be played in solos, duos, trios or squads (four-player teams). When playing in teams each member has specific roles, for example in trios the team is broken down to an In-Game Leader (IGL), Fragger and Support person. During the FNCS Trios in July 2020 Martin and Benjy teamed up with Kevin "Letshe" Fedjuschkin. In their trio, Martin was the IGL and Support, Letshe was the Fragger and Benjy did a little of everything.

Martin, Letshe and Benjy

In-Game Leader (IGL) is the person who fronts the trio. They call the drop-spots, look for enemies, strategise and make the calls within the game.

Fragger is the person who instigates fights to eliminate opponents; they are proactive and take risks to acquire more materials.

Support is the person who scouts for nearby spots for enemies and extra loot. They bring up the rear of the trio, constantly checking behind and guarding flanks.

MULTI-TASKING, REACTION TIMES AND DEXTERITY

If you have ever watched anyone play Fortnite you will have seen that the game is very fast paced especially at the end. Players have to be able to react quickly to the changing in-game situation as well as performing multiple tasks in quick succession. Not only do they have to stay calm and make split-second decisions, but also they have to know where the other players are around them, check their inventory status, scout for information, check zone and game status, as well as eliminate other players. All of this happens in a matter of seconds.

ESPORTS EDUCATION IN THE UK

ESPORTS BUSINESS AND TECHNOLOGY QUALIFICATION (BTEC)

The British Esports Association has recently partnered with Pearson BTEC to create the world's first qualification for young people and adult learners seeking a career in our exciting and rapidly expanding industry. Learners can choose to take either a Level 2 or Level 3 National BTEC qualification.

These new BTEC in Esports qualifications are skills-focused and represent a huge boost to the industry by supporting the creation of clearer career pathways in esports both in the UK and internationally.

As esports continues to boom around the world, demand for people with specific skills such as Public Relations (PR) and Marketing, Shoutcasting and Hosting, Coaching and Production is growing, and these new qualifications developed by Pearson in conjunction with the British Esports Association support those new roles – as well as those wanting to play and grow their career professionally.

SUBJECT UNITS INCLUDE:

- Esports Games, Teams and Tournaments
- Establishing an Esports Organisation
- Streaming for Esports
- Plan for an Esports Event
- Start an Enterprise in Esports
- Design an Esports Game
- Positive Health and Well-being in Esports

ADDITIONAL UNITS
(depending on the course level) include:

- Live-Streamed Broadcasting
- Producing an Esports Brand
- Video Production
- Shoutcasting
- Coaching
- Social Media
- Psychology for Esports Performance
- Ethical and Current Issues in Esports
- Computer Networking

INTERNATIONAL STUDENTS

An International BTEC Level 3 qualification has been launched in esports, so that educational institutions around the world can offer the qualification to overseas students through remote learning.

The units are designed to provide deep insight into esports and will enable students to develop a wide range of transferable skills and knowledge that can be applied to other careers and sectors including digital and careers within science, technology, engineering and mathematics (STEM).

This is especially valuable to students in a changing world where job roles are likely to continually change, and the emphasis is increasingly on flexibility, adaptability and transferable skills.

To ensure that the course content meets industry needs and provides high-quality preparation for progression, the partners engaged experts within esports, educators and employers including the University of Chichester, Sheridans and the North America Scholastic Esports Federation (NASEF).

For more information go to:
www.btec.co.uk/esports

Find out more about the British Esports Association at: www.britishesports.org

Photo credit Jack Frog/Shutterstock.com.

57

CONFETTI INSTITUTE OF CREATIVE TECHNOLOGIES

In September 2020, the Confetti Institute of Creative Technologies, which is part of Nottingham Trent University in the UK, launched a new three-year Esports Production degree course.

Confetti is scheduled to open a brand new, multi-million pound, cutting-edge esports and content creation facility, Confetti X, in autumn 2021 for learning the craft, hosting professional esports events and much more.

ESPORTS PRODUCTION - BACHELOR OF SCIENCES (HONOURS)

On the course, students study the key aspects of the esports industry, including production and broadcast technology, event management, games analysis, entrepreneurship and emerging technologies.

Their world-class live events complex, Metronome, allows for industry-standard live events production. In their brand new £9.1 million digital media hub, students have access to:

- Games studios
- Latest industry-standard software packages
- Hardware suites focused on research and development in Virtual Reality, Augmented Reality and Motion Capture

For more information go to: www.confetti.ac.uk

STAFFORDSHIRE UNIVERSITY

In September 2018, Staffordshire University became the first UK university to offer an esports degree course to their students. The Head of Department for Games and Visual Effects, Dr. Bobbie Fletcher, has been facilitating courses in Gaming, at Staffordshire, since 2004. In 2016, the University accepted a challenge presented by The Association for UK Interactive Entertainment (Ukie) in their white paper, 'Growing the UK as an esports hub'. The report called for an integration of esports into education and in response, both Staffordshire University's Gaming Department and the Business School collaborated to develop dedicated esports Bachelor of Arts (BA) and Master of Art (MA) degrees.

ESPORTS - BACHELOR OF ARTS (HONOURS)

The Bachelor of Arts degree focuses on the business and industry of esports, teaching students in practical technical environments. Students learn how to develop both single player and multi-player team events, create business plans, engage with online communities and promote events through digital marketing.

NSE (National Student Esports) British University Esports Championship Winter Finals, held at Confetti. Photo credit Confetti.

ESPORTS - MASTER OF ARTS (HONOURS)

The Masters degree is designed to develop the research skills needed to work within a growing number of careers and jobs in the esports industry. The focus of the course is on the cultural aspects of esports, influencing policies and practices in the industry and developing a critical awareness of the sociology, legal and political economic landscape.

For more information go to:
www.staffs.ac.uk

Staffordshire University Dedicated Esports Hub. Photo credit Staffordshire University.

ESPORTS GRADUATES

After graduation, Staffordshire University students aim to start their careers in various roles in the esports industry, these include:

BROADCASTING

- On Air Talent
- Technical Management
- Team Management

EVENT PRODUCTION

- Production Crew
- Marketing
- Branding

Their dedicated esports broadcasting hub is a professional standard studio facility designed to broadcast the live transmission of multi-input, competitive gaming tournaments. It houses dedicated presenter and commentator spaces, in addition to the specialist workstations required to deliver a six vs six competitive action.

NORWAY

An increasing number of upper secondary schools (with students aged 16-19) in Norway offer esports as a course within their curriculum. Esports courses feature physical exercise, life skills, diet and the structure of the sport, in addition to skill development in games. Many so-called 'folk high schools' provide general education for young adults without granting academic degrees. Some of these schools offer educational paths within esports, covering subjects like team building and video analysis. Additionally some local traditional sports clubs facilitate esports, offering a LAN-like environment for children to socialise both online and "offline", possibly aiming to bridge the gap between physical sports and esports. The University of Agder offers a full bachelor's degree in academic esports starting in 2022. It is an international program and will be taught in English. The program will cover things like game design, psychology, physical training, programming and finance.

ESPORTS EDUCATION IN EUROPE

There are esports courses offered in other European countries and here is a selection:

 VIDEO GAMES AND ESPORTS MANAGEMENT - BACHELOR'S AND MASTER'S

GAMING BUSINESS SCHOOL (G.BS), FRANCE

G.BS is a management school offering both bachelor's and master's degrees in video game and esports management.

The course trains students for jobs in the video game industry, and more generally in interactive technological media. Their 1,900m² gaming campus in the heart of Lyon, France is dedicated to gaming and learning conditions adapted to the video game sector.

For more information go to:
www.gaming.bs

 ESPORTS MANAGEMENT - BACHELOR OF ARTS

HOCHSCHULE FÜR ANGEWANDTES MANAGEMENT (HAM), GERMANY

The bachelor's degree course at HAM consists of a large number of business courses and modules that are geared towards the esports industry. These include athlete management, brand management, market analysis and market forecasting.

For more information visit:
www.fham.de/studiengaenge/bachelor/esports-management

SPORTS AND ESPORTS MANAGEMENT- BACHELOR OF BUSINESS ADMINISTRATION

GBSB GLOBAL BUSINESS SCHOOL, SPAIN

The GBSB Global Business School offers a Bachelor of Business Administration (BBA) in Sports and Esports Management. The course is designed to give students the skills and knowledge they need to compete in the sports industry and related businesses and organisations. It combines specialist teaching about the principles and practice of sport management, with general training in management, business administration, strategy and research methods. The bachelor's degree helps students to develop a deeper understanding of management, governance, and regulatory issues within the business of sports.

For more information go to:
www.global-business-school.org

 ESPORTS BUSINESS- BACHELOR OF BUSINESS ADMINISTRATION

KAJAANI UNIVERSITY OF APPLIED SCIENCES, FINLAND

Kajaani University of Applied Sciences (KAMK) offers a bachelor's degree in Esports Business specialising in Event Management. The program includes field trips to explore esports events, plus students will also have the opportunity to plan and execute esports events locally.

For more information go to:
www.kamk.fi/en

ESPORTS EDUCATION IN THE USA

COLLEGIATE AND HIGH SCHOOLS

The USA has seen hundreds of schools launch dedicated esports programmes alongside their traditional soccer and football teams.

Through the support of the National Federation of State High School Associations (NFHS) they are able to offer varsity-level high school competition and state championships. Esports, in a similar way to traditional sports, has three tiers of competition: varsity, club and intramurals.

- Intramural sports are the most casual way to join organised athletics.
- Club teams are more competitive, where you play against other schools and require try-outs to join. If you end up on a team, you will work with other skilled students and a coach. Schools tend to sponsor club teams.
- Varsity sports are the most competitive and organised, they are funded by the college or university.

Varsity puts each school's best teams in leagues, with the best team from each school in their state. Each individual state partner crowns a new, official state champion each season. In addition to Fortnite, other esports games are available including: Overwatch, League of Legends, Rocket League and Smite. Students have the opportunity to get a varsity letter in esports, which is an award earned for excellence.

HATHAWAY BROWN

In the USA the Hathaway Brown School in Ohio, an all-girls school, has implemented the first all-female varsity esports program.

ESPORTS SCHOLARSHIPS IN THE USA

The National Association of Collegiate Esports (NACE) is the main governing body for varsity collegiate esports and has awarded millions of dollars in esports scholarships and aid since 2015. There are more than 200 colleges and universities offering nearly 15 million dollars in scholarships per year. NACE are a member-driven organisation who focus on the positive development of esports programs at the collegiate level. They advocate for members to create a strong institutional commitment to esports through varsity programs that include scholarships.

In the USA, NACE is the first association of its kind to promote the education and development of students through sponsored intercollegiate esports programs.

For more information visit:
https://nacesports.org

US ACADEMIC REQUIREMENTS FOR COLLEGE ESPORTS

Since esports are not affiliated with the National Collegiate Athletic Association (NCAA) in the USA, the academic eligibility tends to be more relaxed than with traditional sports. While scholarship requirements vary from school to school, most varsity programs require gamers to maintain a GPA (Grade Point Average) of 2.5 or higher.

NEXT COLLEGE STUDENT ATHLETE (NCSA)

Next College Student Athlete (NCSA) is a college athletic recruiting network that helps student-athletes find their best path to college. NCSA's Esports recruiting guide provides all the information gamers need to know about playing esports in college.

HOW TO GET RECRUITED FOR ESPORTS

To find recruits for their esports teams, college coaches start by performing an initial evaluation of prospects who have submitted a recruiting form. In some cases, coaches also monitor major tournaments to find promising recruits. If a coach is impressed by your Twitch stream or video on demand (VOD), they may invite you to campus to meet current team members and undergo a live try-out.

Try-outs are typically held during or shortly before the school year. They allow the coach to evaluate you in person and test your abilities in a team environment. If you pass the test, the coach may offer you a spot on the team and a partial, full-tuition or full-ride scholarship.

WHAT CAN YOU GET SCHOLARSHIPS FOR?

Varsity programs award esports scholarships to gamers who excel in a wide range of popular titles. Types of games include:

- Multiplayer online battle arena (MOBA): League of Legends (LoL), Dota 2, Heroes of the Storm and Smite.
- First person shooter: Overwatch, Fortnite, Counter-Strike: Global Offensive (CS:GO), PlayerUnknown's Battlegrounds (PUBG) and Paladins.
- Collectable card game: Hearthstone.
- Real-time strategy: StarCraft II.
- Sports games: Rocket League, FIFA and Madden.
- Fighting games: Street Fighter and Mortal Kombat.

For more information go to: www.nacesports.org

HOW MUCH ARE ESPORTS SCHOLARSHIPS?

Esports scholarships are awarded on a school-by-school basis. The majority are partial and seem to range from $500 to $8,000 per year. Several schools are beginning to offer full-tuition, and even full-ride scholarships.

Photo credit **Friends Stock/Shutterstock.com**.

WOMEN IN ESPORTS

In 2020 NBC News reported that only 35 per cent of esports gamers were female, highlighting the fact that women are still in the minority in the esports industry. Efforts are being made to create more diversity and inclusivity through initiatives and opportunities to support women in esports.

In this chapter we hope to give worthy recognition and representation to the female trailblazers in esports, and acknowledge just some of the current opportunities available to women who are looking to start their career in esports.

65

In 2018 Rachell "Valkyrae" Hofstetter was the first female player and content creator to sign with 100 Thieves, and in 2021 she was made a co-owner.

FEMALE FACES OF FORTNITE

Fortnite has a far-reaching appeal to a wide range of players and the game has already produced many female role models. Here are just some of the big names:

LOSERFRUIT

Kathleen "Loserfruit" Belsten is an Australian Fortnite creator. Kathleen is one of the most famous female content creators and has a huge fan following of over 3m subscribers on YouTube.

BROOKEAB

Ashley "BrookeAB" Bond is an American Fortnite player and content creator. Brooke started streaming in July 2018, blew up in May 2019 and joined 100 Thieves in October of the same year. She has since lived in 100 Thieves' content house in Los Angeles with Nadeshot, CouRage and Valkyrae, and has over 350k subscribers on YouTube. She streams a variety of games, plus she paints and cooks and more on stream.

XCHOCOBARS

Janet "xChocoBars" Rose is a Canadian streamer and player, and has 200k+ subscribers on YouTube. In 2018, Janet finished in second place in the Fortnite Fall Skirmish, and in 2019 she was a finalist for the Twitch Streamer of the Year award at the 11th Shorty Awards.

POOKIEFACE

Sarah "Pookieface" Lynn is a Twitch host and commentator. In February 2020 Sarah hosted the Secret Skirmish Fortnite Tournament together with Kristen "KittyPlays" Valnicek, forming the first female casting duo at a major esports event.

LULU

Lyndsey "LuluLovely", or simply "Lulu", is a Fortnite streamer and content creator from Texas, USA. Lyndsey gained popularity for playing Apex Legends and was referred to as the 'Queen of Apex Legends' for her gameplay skills; she even hosted her own tournament. In November 2019 she signed as a content creator for NRG; she produces Fortnite content amongst other videos.

SOMMERSET

Kayla "Sommerset" is an American Fortnite streamer and content creator. After just four months of streaming, Kayla was made a Twitch Partner and now has over 400k followers. In July 2020 Kayla signed up with the esports organisation, Luminosity Gaming as part of their content team.

KITTYPLAYS

Kristen "KittyPlays" Valnicek is a Twitch streamer and YouTuber. Kristen started out playing CS:GO and Dota 2 before she discovered Fortnite. She hosts and produces her own show "Playtime with KittyPlays", where she interviews and plays games with celebrities to entertain her 600k+ YouTube subscribers. In 2018, Kristen won the Korean Open Duos Tournament with Turner "Tfue" Tenney, and the following year she was an official host and caster at the Fortnite World Cup in New York.

In 2021, Emily "Perkz" Perkins, a school teacher in the UK, rose to fame as an esports content creator, after her Twitter handle was mistaken for the League of Legends professional player Luka "Perkz" Perković. Emily – who used to game as a hobby – now produces content for the esports organisation Cloud 9, promoting inclusivity and diversity within the community.

ALL-FEMALE FORTNITE TEAM

In 2018 the esports organisation Gen.G announced that they would be signing the first ever all-female Fortnite team including duo players Tina "Tinaraes" Perez and Maddie "Maddiesuun" Mann.

TINARAES

Tina "Tinaraes" Perez is an American professional Fortnite player. Tina grew up in Texas, USA, and the first console she played on was a Nintendo 64. Tina won the Fortnite Rivals Tournament at TwitchCon 2019, with players Keenan "Rhux" Santos and Julio "Pika" Cesar Nevarez.

MADDIESUUN

Maddie "Maddiesuun" Mann is a professional Fortnite player from Massachusetts, USA. She has always been competitive; starting out playing soccer she switched to gaming when she started playing PUBG. In February 2020 Maddie competed at DreamHack Anaheim; unfortunately she missed out on qualifying for the semi-finals due to a technical issue in the first stage of the competition.

HISTORY IN THE MAKING

In February 2020, Gen.G signed Moqii, a 14-year-old female Swedish professional Fortnite player. She made history in the Solo FNCS Qualifier 2 in July 2020, where she became the first ever female winner of an event. Moqii has been playing Fortnite and placing in tournaments since March 2019 and participating in LAN events including DreamHack Anaheim 2020, which Martin won. Gen.G has later moved on from Fortnite to Valorant.

ALL-FEMALE TOURNAMENTS

WOMEN OF THE ERENA (WOTE)

Women of the Erena is an all-female tournament series hosted by eFuse, in partnership with ESPN Esports, featuring a selection of the best female talent in gaming. In 2020 the WOTE series featured a Fortnite Duos Tournament that saw the champions share a $20,000 prize pool.

THE NATIONAL UNIVERSITY ESPORTS LEAGUE

The National University Esports League (NUEL) is an esports league for university students in the UK, bringing together teams to represent their university in: League of Legends, Hearthstone, CS:GO, Overwatch and Rocket League. September 2020 saw the first women's League of Legends tournament, which was open to all female students in the UK.

WOMEN IN ESPORTS SCHOLARSHIP

The University of Roehampton in London, UK, offers a Women in Esports scholarship, which is the first women-focused esports scholarship to be introduced in Europe. The programme aims to improve diversity and inclusivity in the esports industry and to inspire the next generation of women esports professionals.

DREAMHACK SHOWDOWN

In May 2019, DreamHack partnered with ZOWIE and Esports-Management to launch DreamHack Showdown, an all-female Counter-Strike: Global Offensive (CS:GO) competition. The LAN tournament was held in Valencia in July 2019 with a prize pool of $100K. In advance of the tournament, LAN qualifiers were held in Shanghai, China during the ZOWIE Divina Women's Asian CS:GO Championship with online qualifiers in North America and Europe.

ESPORTS ORGANISATIONS – ALL-FEMALE ROSTERS

There are now several all-women professional teams including:

XSET–CS:GO

Cloud9 White–Valorant

Dignitas–Valorant and CS:GO

TSM–Valorant

Gen.G–Valorant

GUILD X–Valorant

GXR–CS:GO,
League of Legends and Valorant

BRITISH ESPORTS ASSOCIATION

In late 2019, the British Esports Association launched an initiative to celebrate women within the esports industry. The Women in Esports initiative aims to create a welcoming community which encourages more female players to take part in esports tournaments at any level. Through this initiative, British Esports wants to help raise awareness and improve inclusivity in esports, similarly to other organisations such as Women in Games/Women in Esports, Women of Esports, AnyKey, FemaleLegends and more.

GIRLGAMER ESPORTS FESTIVAL

The GIRLGAMER Esports Festival is the world's leading event to celebrate and promote women's competitiveness in esports, as well as a platform to promote women empowerment through competitions, gender inclusive activations, awareness conferences and a docuseries titled "Now is our Time". Teams come together to compete in Counter-Strike: Global Offensive and League of Legends.

Photo credit GIRLGAMER.

MAMABENJYFISHY PLAYS FORTNITE

Anne: 'Playing Fortnite and streaming was not something that I have ever planned or envisaged I would ever do. I first tried playing Fortnite just to see what it was like in Chapter 2 Season 4 at the end of 2020 but only played for a few hours and didn't get very far so never pursued it further. I was always busy working and was happy just watching other people play.

At the start of 2021 Benjy started playing chess and was invited to take part in the PogChamps3 Tournament. Benjy reached out to Jon Ludvig Hammer, a Grand Master from Oslo, who is an acquaintance of Johnny's. I watched Benjy's daily lessons with Jon Ludvig, which were streamed online. Jon is also a keen Fortnite player and occasionally would play Fortnite after the chess lessons. I stayed online to watch his stream. Having only really watched professional players stream Fortnite it was refreshing to see someone who was not so proficient at playing having a go and just enjoying playing the game without worrying too much about the outcome. This was my inspiration to give Fortnite another go.

I tried to use a keyboard and mouse but that didn't work for me as I suffer from repetitive strain injury (RSI). So, Benjy lent me a controller and suggested that I tried that. I still found it very confusing because of all the different buttons to switch between but after a while I managed to work out what to press – even if I wasn't that good at it! I made it my goal to get to the Champion League in Chapter 2 Season 5 (December 2020 to March 2021) as a solo player. I went on to play some of the solo cash cups, playing strategically for placements rather than through eliminations.'

STREAMING ON TWITCH

Anne: 'In March 2021, I decided to start streaming on Twitch. I was nervous when I first started as I wasn't sure quite what I was doing, and I had to get a lot of help from Benjy.

I made the mistake of not having moderators on my channel during my first ever stream! The chat went crazy which was very stressful, but thankfully I managed to rectify this and I now have a fantastic team behind me. I soon became a Twitch Partner and started to stream for around 100 hours a month. By July 2021 I had reached 500k hours watched on my channel. I also stream Fortnite through my Discord group where I go to chat and connect, and play other games.'

COMPETITIVE FORTNITE

Anne: 'During Chapter 2 Season 6 (March to June 2021) I teamed up with my duo partner Bella (@igirlybella) who I also trio with, along with a variety of other team-mates. Bella has played an important part in my progress, helping and encouraging me to improve along with my moderators Scott (@SC0TTAH) and PhoeniixReii (@LionheartOhMy) who have all become close friends. I enjoy taking part in all the tournaments and my aim is to qualify through the open round of FNCS and to be able to progress further into the tournament, maybe even one day being able to compete against Benjy in the finals!'

SIGNING WITH GALAXY RACER ESPORTS (GXR)

Anne: 'In September 2021 after competing in the Aubameyang Cup with Bella, GXR offered me the opportunity to join their organisation as a content creator. I became the first mum to sign with an esports organisation which is amazing! I am keen to be a positive role model in the esports community, to encourage more inclusivity and to demonstrate to other parents all the positive aspects of gaming. In the future, I am also looking forward to playing competitively for GXR in various cash cups and FNCS tournaments.'

Anne at her workplace at home as a content creator for Galaxy Racer. Photo credit Emily Mudie Photography.

SOCIAL MEDIA FOLLOWING SEPTEMBER 2021

TWITCH 429K

INSTAGRAM 90K

TWITTER 105K

YOUTUBE 165K

TIKTOK 113K

IRINA "REDDYSH / RED"

Full-time Fortnite streamer and content creator from Romania

Irina was born and raised in Bucharest, Romania. Before committing full time to streaming and content creation, Irina worked in the marketing department at Google. In 2019, after only six months of streaming Fortnite, she became a Twitch Partner.

CAN YOU TELL US ABOUT YOURSELF?

Red: 'I've always loved gaming. I grew up playing on a PC and I play Fortnite. I'm mostly known for my red hair, strong accent and crazy pump flicks. When I partnered on Twitch after only six months of streaming Fortnite I knew this was the right path for me. I would say that my stream is one of the most positive places one can find on the Internet, mainly because of my community – my amazing Red Squad.'

HAVE YOU ALWAYS BEEN INTERESTED IN GAMING? WHAT ARE SOME OF THE OTHER GAMES YOU HAVE PLAYED?

Red: 'When I was growing up, my family never owned a console. We got a PC when I was six and I then tried out a lot of games. When I was seven, I switched from playing Barbie and other 'kids' games' to playing Counter-Strike: Source, and ended up playing for many years. I always had a good aim on mouse and keyboard, to the point where I used to be kicked off CS servers because people thought I had hacks – that gave me a lot of confidence. What I loved the most about CS was that I could team up with my family. We used to have Skype group calls with my brother, uncle, cousins – all of us playing together. Nowadays, I play Fortnite 98 per cent of the time, but I really like Valorant too, or trying out new games like It Takes Two which I absolutely adore.'

WHAT IS IT ABOUT FORTNITE THAT YOU ENJOY AND WHAT SEASON DID YOU START?

Red: 'I started playing Fortnite in Season 4, back in May 2018. I love the building aspect more than anything. It's still fascinating to me what our brains can do to adapt in various situations, all the buttons we press, the decisions we make so quickly. I have a dual PC setup, so streaming doesn't affect my game and I love showing my community my improvement, and I often stream creative sessions too.'

WAS IT DIFFICULT TO MAKE THE DECISION TO QUIT YOUR MARKETING JOB AT GOOGLE AND START STREAMING FULL-TIME?

Red: 'For exactly two years I managed a dream job with streaming: coming back from work at 7pm, and streaming from 9pm until 1:30 am every single day (I've always had a super consistent schedule). The decision to go full-time with streaming was not hard, because everyone around me has been supportive. My community, family, even my manager and everyone from work wanted my stream to be successful. I had enough savings to cover the cost of my rent for at least a few months, so that's when I knew I was ready for the big step. I did a really good job at Google, but honestly I love this content creation world too much to ever go back to working a 9–6 job.'

Q YOU STREAM FOR APPROXIMATELY SIX HOURS MOST DAYS, DO YOU FIND IT HARD TO COME UP WITH CONTENT IDEAS AND COLLABORATIONS?

Red: 'I have a consistent schedule, streaming every single day except for Wednesdays (my only day off) and I try to do content and collabs at least once per week. For me, there are two types of streams: streams that are special and well planned in advance, like the Subathon event that I did for my second Partnerversary – it was a 71 hours stream filled with lots of activities. Then other streams that are spontaneous and not planned at all, like when I stream together with Anne or Squatingdog, or when Fortnite cancelled a cash cup and I organised a tournament for my trio. We used the same points format on that day and there were prizes. Even when I play, let's say arena, I try my best to make it entertaining. At the end of the day, it's all about the vibes in the community and interactions and I'm lucky that they never put pressure on me and show me that no matter how I play or what I do (it could even be a different game), they're still there for me and for the Red Squad. That's why streams where I just hit the go live button, without any collab or specific content in mind, turn out great.'

Q DO YOU HAVE A FAVOURITE EVENT/TOURNAMENT THAT YOU HAVE COMPETED IN?

Red: 'The hype that FNCS and DreamHack create is just something else. Everyone is rooting for us, we always end up getting wins. I can see through the corner of my eye when people cheer for every single elimination we get. It's wild and a true emotional rollercoaster. I love trio and duo tourneys the most. I've participated in two Twitch Rivals events so far – Nick Eh's and Sypher's – which I absolutely loved. I had the time of my life knowing that I get to be involved alongside streamers I look up to.'

Q YOU HAVE BEEN PLAYING IN THE VARIOUS CASH CUPS AND FNCS TOURNAMENTS. HAVE YOU CONSIDERED BECOMING A PROFESSIONAL PLAYER AND COMPETING?

Red: 'I've always been a competitive person, so from the moment I played my first tournament in August 2020 I just couldn't stop. I finally came to the conclusion that I do belong in the Fortnite competitive world. If people want to watch pro gameplay in a tournament, they can watch Benjy or the other pros. But if they want to watch a girl who's trying to make her way to her first competitive earnings, improving from season to season, ending up clutching FNCS qualifier wins and growing as a player, together with people she met through her community, they can watch me! It's been an amazing journey and I'm curious where it will take me.'

Q WOULD YOU CONSIDER SIGNING FOR AN ORGANISATION?

Red: 'It would be an honour, but I don't want to rush it. I want to be worthy of it. I'm a people person and I love collabs, so I feel like we would come up with incredible content if I joined a family. Maybe one day!'

Q ARE THERE ANY CHALLENGES YOU HAVE ENCOUNTERED STREAMING?

Red: 'Of course – especially as a girl in the streaming world! There are people who assume a lot of bad things about us, but I like proving them wrong. I have an incredible community and mods who keep me safe, so if someone tries to be toxic in a chat, most of the time I don't even get to see it. We are a family friendly community, so this has also helped keep the environment safe, as we don't allow people to cross the line.'

Q **WHAT ARE YOUR TIPS FOR ASPIRING CONTENT CREATORS?**

Red: 'I always emphasise the importance of organisation and consistency. People need to know what days you're streaming and the hour. And always try to remember that people are there for you as well as for the gameplay.'

Photo credit Reddysh.

DISABILITY IN ESPORTS

Gaming and esports want to break down the barriers in competitive sport using new technology to create a more equal playing field, to allow players with physical and cognitive disabilities to compete with their peers.

GAMERS WITH DISABILITIES

According to research from the charity AbleGamers, up to 46 million gamers in the United States have some sort of disability that affects them playing video games. Research from Muscular Dystrophy UK found that one in three disabled gamers have been forced to stop playing due to their disability.

CUSTOM SETUPS

Charities such as SpecialEffect and AbleGamers are helping to find ways for people to play video games using custom gaming setups and high-tech gadgets, such as mouth controllers or voice control.

GUNMA ESPORTS FESTIVAL JAPAN

On the 31st August 2019 the Gunma Esports Festival in Japan held its first ever disabled-friendly League of Legends tournament. Four teams of five players competed for a prize of one million yen (approx. £7000 or $9000). The festival aimed to bridge the gap between able-bodied gamers and disabled competitors, with plans to create a competition featuring both groups in the future.

MICROSOFT XBOX ADAPTIVE CONTROLLER

SpecialEffect and AbleGamers have worked alongside Microsoft along with the Cerebral Palsy Foundation, Warfighter Engaged, and many community members, to design the Xbox Adaptive Controller.

This controller has been designed to meet the needs of gamers with limited mobility, featuring large programmable buttons which connect to external switches to help make gaming more accessible.

Microsoft Xbox adaptive controller. Photo credit SpecialEffect.

FORTNITE ACCESSIBILITY FEATURES

Color Blind Mode: Fortnite includes three settings based on a player's type of colour vision deficiency. From the Accessibility menu, players may select one of three types of Color Blind Modes: Protanope, Deuteranope, or Tritanope. Additionally, players may further adjust the Color Blind Settings of the game with the Color Blind Strength Slider.

Visualisation: Within Fortnite there are visualisation options for every essential sound in the game, which enables a player to be able to see treasure chests, footsteps/running and gunfire. It also lets the player know the approximate direction and distance. You can in addition set Color Blind mode and accommodate input when using accessible controls.

EWOK SIGNS TO FAZE

FaZe "Ewok" is a Fortnite content creator who was born deaf and uses sound visualiser effects during matches. Ewok rose to fame after being hosted on Timothy "TimTheTatman" Betar's Twitch stream. Then, at the age of 13, Ewok was signed by FaZe and competed in the 2019 Fortnite ProAm Summer Block Party.

BLINKVII – RICKY THE FORTNITE PLAYER WITH NO HANDS

Ricky "Blink VII" Williams was born without hands and is truly an inspirational player in the Fortnite world. He started gaming when he was young on his Nintendo 64 and later played Call of Duty II on the PlayStation. In 2018, Ricky rose to fame after he posted a very motivational video about himself, "Meet Blink, The Fortnite Player With No Hands". He believes that anyone can overcome adversity, and achieve whatever they want to in life by having a strong mental attitude.

Ricky started playing Fortnite on an Xbox with a wired controller, using a combination of arm and leg movement. After being inspired by Ali "Myth" Kabbani's gameplay, Ricky made the switch to PC using mouse and keyboard controls. His talents don't end with gaming as he is also an amazing graphic design artist. Ricky now has over 200k YouTube subscribers and continues to inspire players all over the world.

Ricky. Photo credit @BlinkVII.

Photo credit @BlinkVII.

SPECIALEFFECT – THE GAMERS' CHARITY

The UK-based charity SpecialEffect has been working on more inclusion for people with physical disabilities, by helping them to play video games. Their website says 'it's everyone's turn to play video games' and they have been creating custom gaming setups so that no one is left out of gaming. By working with hardware and software developers, using a range of technology from adapted controllers to eye-control, gamers of all ages are given the opportunity to play and compete.

Here are just a few of the inspirational stories of people SpecialEffect have helped:

MEET BECKY

Becky: 'I can't do a lot but I can play video games on my own, which gives me a sense of independence and achievement.'

Becky has severe quadriplegic cerebral palsy. She can't use her arms or hands, but she can control an eye movement tracking device. Through this she can immerse herself in Minecraft with the help of EyeMine, a special software created by the charity that gives her full control over all aspects of the game.

MEET CHARLIE

Charlie's father: 'Helping Charlie's imagination run wild in games also helps in fine-tuning his motor skills, multitasking, problem solving and hand-eye coordination.'

Charlie's finally able to enjoy the games he's spent so long watching other people play, thanks to a custom controller setup devised by SpecialEffect's specialist assessment team. He struggles to coordinate his arms due to cerebral palsy but his setup, which includes several large button switches to replicate the controller buttons, a large joystick and secure mounting equipment, makes games easier for him to play.

MEET PAUL

Paul, who has a spinal injury and can't use his hands, plays Fortnite with his shoulder, hand, head, mouth and voice. He controls a PC really well with a head-controlled mouse and a couple of switches that utilise his shoulder and arm movement, and now uses over 40 voice commands in Fortnite after discovering a tutorial video on the SpecialEffect's GameAccess website.

Paul: 'After my accident I gave up hope of playing as I never thought I'd be able to keep up, then I stumbled across the SpecialEffect video and it changed my life.'

For more information go to:
www.specialeffect.org.uk

EYE GAZE GAMES

SpecialEffect also run the
www.eyegazegames.com website,
which contains games that can be
played normally but also have settings
that can be specifically optimised for
disabled people who use eye control.

Global chess challenge: Kati in Finland plays chess against Lucinda in Sussex through the Eye Gaze website. Both have little or no body movement and use eye-controlled computers as a way to play games and access technology.

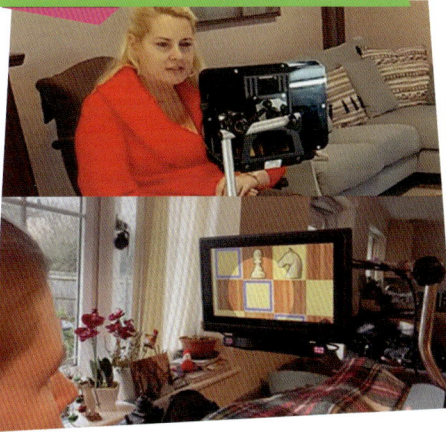

INSOMNIA GAMING EXPOS

You can experience gameplay with some of SpecialEffect's accessible gaming setups at the Insomnia gaming expos. SpecialEffect are a charity partner at the event.

All photos credit to SpecialEffect.

2019 FORTNITE WORLD CUP

After ten qualification weeks, the top one hundred solo players and the top 50 duo teams from around the world came to compete in the biggest event of its type ever staged, the Fortnite World Cup. The inaugural event took place at the Arthur Ashe Stadium, home of the US Open tennis tournament, in Queens, New York City, between 26th and 28th July 2019.

13TH APRIL TO 21ST JUNE 2019

Ten weekends of online qualifiers, alternately solos and duos

THURSDAY 25TH JULY 2019

Players' tour at Arthur Ashe Stadium and live press conference

FRIDAY 26TH JULY 2019

Creative Finals and Pro-Am Event

SATURDAY 27TH JULY 2019

Duo Finals

SUNDAY 28TH JULY 2019

Solo Finals

Benjy and Martin displayed on a big screen at the Arthur Ashe Stadium. Photo credit benjyfishy.

WORLD CUP QUALIFICATION

Anne: 'The decision to lower the age restriction of the Fortnite World Cup in 2019 gave Benjy the chance to compete in the tournament. It was one of the most memorable times in his career to date, as it was his first major live competitive tournament (which is also known as a LAN). Benjy along with Klaus "Stompy" Konstanzer became the first two players in Fortnite history to qualify for both the World Cup Solo and Duos competition. Benjy and Martin were two of only eighteen players to double qualify for both events.'

Johnny: 'It had been a long five months from when the competition was announced in February 2019 to the finals in July. The ten weeks of qualifying had been a nerve-wracking experience for everyone and at times very challenging, especially as Martin didn't qualify for the finals in the first week. However, Martin seemed to take it in his stride and bounced back. He managed to qualify for the duos competition, with Benjy, in week 2 and the solo competition in week 5. Finally we could then breathe a sigh of relief.'

> **Third and qualified! See you in NYC.**
> *Benjy*

#1	**E11 Stompy**	**74 PTS**
#2	**TQ PrisiOn3rO**	**72 PTS**
#3	**NRG benjyfishy**	**68 PTS**
#4	**Gambit.letw1k3**	**66 PTS**

> **HOLY LASAD-ASDGASD LETS GO!**
> *Martin*

#1	**Atlantis Letshe**	**87 PTS**
#2	**AGO JarkoS**	**67 PTS**
#3	**N47 Klusia**	**66 PTS**
#4	**NRG MrSavageM**	**65 PTS**

DUOS

EU RESULTS

WEEK 2 FINALS

#1

NRG BENJYFISHY

NRG MRSAVAGEM

$10,000

LONDON BOOTCAMP

Anne: 'During the qualifying weeks and time leading up to departing for New York, Benjy had the opportunity to visit the London headquarters of esports organisation Fnatic, where he got to meet more of his gaming friends IRL, including another well-known UK Fortnite player, Kyle "Mongraal" Jackson. Esports fosters camaraderie and friendship between the players and teams, and even though neither Benjy nor Kyle are signed with Fnatic, they were both made to feel very welcome. Benjy also joined Kyle at a weekend bootcamp in London hosted by another esports organisation, Cooler Esports, where they could practise in the weeks leading up to the World Cup Grand Finals.'

FILMING PLAYER PROFILES

Anne: 'During the preceding weeks to the finals, we were approached by Epic Games to ask if Benjy was interested in being filmed for the Fortnite player profiles videos. Epic also wanted to feature Benjy and Martin together in a duos video, which they both agreed to. The dates were set and the film crew arranged to fly out from the US to film Benjy's solo video, followed by the duos section with Martin and Johnny, who would also fly to the UK. I was apprehensive about appearing on camera, as it's not something that comes naturally to either Benjy or myself. Any apprehension quickly evaporated as the producer Beth Sciallis and her professional film crew put us completely at our ease. I would say that I count the filming process as one of the special moments leading up to the tournament.'

Johnny: 'A few days later, the crew filmed Martin and his big brother Mikael back home in Oslo, Norway. It was quite surreal to open our home for three days to a crew of five people. They were very nice and professional, and it turned out to be a memorable experience.'

If you want to watch the videos search for 'Fortnite World Cup Player Profiles' on YouTube. The duo video is available at https://vimeo.com/425247163.

Photo credit benjyfishy.

FRIDAY FORTNITE

Anne: 'During the filming process, Benjy and Martin took part in an online duo tournament called Friday Fortnite and streaming on Twitch was an essential component. Unfortunately we didn't have sufficient internet capacity at our house and therefore we had to quickly make other arrangements. Luckily I managed to find a local computer shop, called CLD Computers, who were willing to help us.

Thankfully the owner, Luke Davies, allowed Benjy and Martin private use of the shop's gaming centre so the boys could compete. Luke has been helping Benjy with his computer setup ever since.

The film crew also came with us to film some shots of the boys practising together. The footage featured in the Benjyfishy and MrSavage duo profile film, which premiered during the World Cup Finals. After filming with us all day, which included an early start, the exhausted film crew left us about 8pm to fly to Oslo to prepare for filming Martin at his home.'

Johnny: 'The Friday Fortnite tournament was based on a bracket system, with duos playing in a best-of-two format within a double-elimination bracket (winner's and loser's). The duo with the most eliminations after two games moved on to the next round. The final was between the finalists of the winner's and loser's brackets. The games took place alternately on EU and NA servers to balance out differences in ping delay and lag between EU and NA teams.'

Anne: 'One of the positive sides to Fortnite is how palpable the strong community spirit is among the players and the support they offer each other. For example, during the tournament NRG Williams "Zayt" Aubin tweeted his words of encouragement during one of the matches, as the boys definitely needed the support.

Benjy and Martin managed to beat Issa "Issa" Rahim and Liam "Kamo" Fillery (both members of Ghost Gaming Europe at the time) in the winner's bracket final.'

> **"Thanks to cld.solutions** for allowing Benjy and I to use their gaming center in Surrey so that I could stream the Friday Fortnite tournament last Friday. **"**
> *Martin*

From left to right: Chris Teitsworth, Benjy, Martin and Luke Davies. Photo credit MrSavage.

> **"TAKE MY ENERGY, Benjyfishy MrSavage. "**
> Zayt

> **"ok we won now gg thanks zayt. "**
> Benjy

Benjy and Martin during the Friday Fortnite tournament, 1st June 2019.
Photo credit benjyfishy.

Anne: 'We were all exhausted, running on adrenalin and completely oblivious to the fact that a duo must win two rounds of the winner's bracket finals to be crowned the winner. So, when Benjy and Martin defeated Issa and Kamo, our celebrations were premature and we discovered that the boys had to play another round. At the end of the first game Issa and Kamo said to them, "It's not over yet, what are you guys doing? It's not over, you have to win twice, you came from the loser's bracket – did you think you already won?"

I'm not sure how, but the duo remarkably managed to summon all the energy they could muster to play again and they won! Claiming victory around 5.30am.'

❝ *We got it, we definitely got it this time!* ❞
Benjy

❝ *Friday Fortnite was probably one of the hardest tournaments that I have ever played just because of how exhausting it was, as it was so long.* ❞
Martin

Johnny: 'After the tournament, we managed to get back and get a few hours of sleep, but Benjy and Martin both had to be back at the gaming centre the following day, as they wanted to compete in the week 8 duo World Cup qualifiers. Unsurprisingly, the boys didn't do as well as they had hoped and failed to qualify for the Sunday finals. Parents and players should both be aware that playing at a competitive level for long periods of time is not something that can be sustained.'

MrSavage

@MrSavage

QUALIFYING REGION

EUROPE

HOME COUNTRY

NORWAY

FORTNITE
WORLD CUP

 **benjyfishy**

@benjyfishy

QUALIFYING REGION

EUROPE

HOME COUNTRY

UNITED KINGDOM

PLAYER FACT

Both players qualified for solo and duos. benjyfishy was one of the first players to qualify for both.

NEW YORK

Johnny: 'Both Benjy and Martin were due to attend a bootcamp with other NRG players prior to the World Cup tournament, therefore we arrived in New York City a few days early. Martin and I travelled with Peter, and we coordinated our journey with Benjy and Anne to make sure we arrived on the same day as they did.'

Anne: 'Benjy and I were fortunate to travel with Benjy's brother, Charles, and Charles' girlfriend Amina. This allowed us a chance to spend some valuable family time and to share this incredible adventure together. It was the first time that Benjy had ever been to the USA, so even flying was a big adventure. On arrival, the first thing that was noticeable was the heat, which is something we don't really experience too often in the UK. Upon checking into the hotel one of the really cool first impressions was the key-cards for the rooms, which were overlaid with Fortnite characters.'

Johnny: 'Some of Martin's family members travelled to the USA to support him. This included his older brother Mikael, grandmother Anne Mari, uncle Gøran, and cousins Jørgen Mathias and Jacob. All the World Cup players were booked into the same hotel, the Grand Hyatt on 42nd Street in New York City. The lobby of the hotel was the focal point of the experience, as all the players could be seen chilling in the lobby, along with fans who would congregate to get an opportunity to see their idols and get pictures and autographs.'

HELIX ESPORTS CENTER

Anne: 'After checking into our hotel, we made our way to the Helix eSports Center in New Jersey, which had been booked as a practice centre for the whole NRG team, in the days leading up to the final. The centre was extremely well set up, as NRG players had their own designated room. There were also other rooms assigned to teams, including Ghost Gaming and Solary. Having since travelled to other LAN events around the world, we did not appreciate at the time how good this bootcamp was compared to some of the others we have subsequently experienced. We felt very welcome and it was a great opportunity to meet some of the other teams, players and their parents.'

Benjy with brother Charles and his girlfriend Amina. Photo credit benjyfishy.

Martin's family: L to R: Anne Mari (grandmother), Martin, Jacob (cousin), Jørgen Mathias (cousin), Mikael (brother), Gøran (uncle), Johnny. Photo credit MrSavage.

Outside the Helix eSports Center. From left to right: Benjy, Murph Vandervelde, Patrick Kenyon, Martin. Photo credit benjyfishy.

MEET AND GREET

Johnny: 'The World Cup week also saw Benjy and Martin's first Meet and Greet event, which was sponsored by Nathan's Hot Dogs on 368 Broadway in New York City. None of us really knew what to expect and would anyone even show? Our fears were soon dispelled as there were fans queuing around the block to get a chance to meet the boys along with the rest of the NRG players. Little things like perfecting an autograph in a hurry is something you don't really think too much about.'

NRG FAM GET TOGETHER

Johnny: 'The days leading up to the World Cup primarily consisted of copious amounts of practice for the boys, almost 24/7, with the occasional opportunity to chill and relax. One such occasion was when everyone got together for the NRG family dinner, where we finally got to meet other members of the team in person and the people behind the organisation. We met Brett Lautenbach (President), Andy Miller (Founder and CEO), Jaime Cohenca (General Manager) and Grady Rains (Executive Producer).

Anne: 'We all enjoyed the NRG family dinner and get together. The players were given memento of the occasion in the form of a Gucci wallet.'

Benjy and Martin meeting fans queuing outside the 'Meet and greet'. Photo credit NRG.

❝ **NRG are really supportive and always have our backs. I got to meet everyone who works for NRG a few days ago, and they're all super nice people.** ❞

Martin

Gathered at the NRG family dinner in New York City.

From left to right: EpicWhale, Jaime, Anne, Benjy, Charles, Amina, Johnny, Brett, Peter, Mike (EpicWhale's dad), Andy, Zayt, Martin, Grady, Symfuhny. Photo credit NRG.

SOLARY NO-BUILD CHALLENGE

Anne: 'Whilst at the Helix eSports Center, Benjy and Martin participated in the #NoBuildChallenge tournament streamed by the French esports organisation, Solary, in cooperation with World Wild Fund for Nature (WWF). I found this to be a particularly poignant moment, as it was the first time that Benjy did a facecam live on stream. Up until that point Benjy had only used either a mouse or keyboard cam, so this was a big deal for him.'

Martin outside the 'Meet and greet' posing together with fans. Photo credit NRG.

Martin, Yoshi, Kinstaar and Benjy taking part in the Solary #NoBuildChallenge. Photo credit benjyfishy.

A memorable moment at the Helix eSports Center was when Benjy and Martin took on the challenge to break the Fortnite Pinata Llama. Photo credit benjyfishy.

PLAYERS' LOUNGE

Johnny: 'The event itself was well organised by Epic Games, but flew past in a bit of a whirlwind. The boys put a lot of pressure on themselves as did all the players participating and everyone had high expectations that they were going to do well. The nature of professional players in any sport or discipline is to be goal orientated to win and be the best; Benjy and Martin are no exception to this rule. This ultimately puts extra pressure and stress on us as parents, as you want to support your children to achieve their best.'

Anne: 'The tournament took place at the Arthur Ashe Stadium over the course of three days. In addition, there was a walk-through preview day for everyone, combined with a media day for the press before the competition. In the players' lounge, I was very excited and star struck to see some of esports' biggest names like Ninja, Tfue and the casters including Sund0wn. Benjy wasn't fazed at all. He was just excited to finally be at the event.'

Anne: 'The film crew that had come to our houses were also doing the filming at the event. We were all slowly getting used to having cameras feet away from us watching our every move, although it was still a little daunting. Amongst all the uncertainty, I felt a sense of calm reassurance to see the familiar faces that we had spent time with during the summer, and this helped to calm our nerves for the events that were to follow. To be able to thank them in person for all the work they had done on the finished profile videos was very special. Both Johnny and I were very emotional watching the videos for the first time. Words can't convey how tremendously proud I am of Benjy's achievements at such a young age.'

From left to right: Tfue, Zayt, Benjy, Bizzle, Symfuhny, Endretta's dad Erik, Martin, Endretta, EpikWhale.

Benjy, Mongraal and Martin. Photo credit MrSavage.

Benjy and Martin at the official press conference. They were two among the five selected players invited. Photo credit Nick Dotto (@NickyDotz).

> " It's always been a goal to qualify for a major tournament and be able to compete in it. "
>
> *Benjy*

PRESS CONFERENCE

Before the start of the 2019 Fortnite World Cup, a press conference was held featuring some of the top competitors at the event, including Benjy and Martin. They were asked questions about their thoughts ahead of the tournament. They both handled the questions well and were not overwhelmed by the experience.

What is motivating each of you in this tournament?

Benjy: 'Getting to this point is really big for me. It's always been a goal to qualify for a major tournament and be able to compete in it. Now that I've achieved that, I think my goal is to be known as one of the best players in the world.'

Martin: 'I feel like I've already won just being able to meet everyone I've been talking to. It's been one of the best experiences of my life. I feel like the prize pool is just a bonus.'

How did your friends and family react to your career choice?

Benjy: 'I remember I won a $20,000 tournament a few months ago with MrSavage, and that was the first money I had ever won from playing the game. I told my friends at school and they couldn't believe it. They thought I was lying at first, so I had to show them the clip of me winning. All of my friends and family have been really supportive.'

Martin: 'I'm really grateful for my family's support, because they're really, really supportive of what I do.'

Benjy and Martin being interviewed by the BBC (British Broadcasting Corporation) before the 2019 Fortnite World Cup finals. Photo credit MrSavage.

FINALS

Anne: 'Friday saw the World Cup Pro-Am event and Creative finals take place, which we could have attended, but as the boys were keen to get in some last-minute practice we decided to watch it on the television at the Helix eSports Center. None of us managed to get much sleep the night before the first final, which was the duo competition.

The excitement was electric when we arrived at the stadium the next day. All the emotions of the last few months had culminated in the events about to unfold during the next few hours. I remember being an emotional wreck as I kept bursting out crying. It took me a while to calm down. I think the expectation that Benjy and Martin were one of the favourites to win played a role in this.'

Johnny: 'If the boys were feeling nervous on the inside, they certainly didn't give us any hints of their stress. I guess they were fuelled by the excitement of the event. Martin later said that he wasn't nervous as he felt that he had prepared himself as best as he could for the competition. To prevent cheating, Epic Games had provided all players with pre-checked mice, keyboards, and headsets, which were waiting for them at their seats.

All players were supposed to get their personal choice of mouse and keyboard, since changing these is something that can take weeks to adjust to, if ever. But due to an error that didn't happen for all players. Benjy and Martin were lucky and got their equipment.'

Anne: 'To be honest, the whole event flew by in a bit of a haze. When I asked Benjy to describe his games, he said he really couldn't remember much and that it must be the adrenaline rush. I remember the first game specifically, as Benjy and Martin had high ground. Benjy was still alive in end game and I got very excited. They were in 5th place after the 1st game but to be honest the rest of the games were a bit of a blur. They ended up finishing in 14th position overall, but despite this great achievement they were very disappointed and determined to focus on the solos happening the following day.'

Johnny: 'Martin went straight back to the Helix eSports Center that evening to switch mode and practise solos. Their experience in the duos helped them ahead of the solos competition the next day, as they knew what it felt like to play in that huge stadium. Being double qualified as they both were meant they could keep their seats, which provided them some assurance.'

Benjy (to the right) entering the stage for the solo finals. Photo credit MrSavage.

Benjy and Martin at their player seats during the World Cup finals. Photo credit MrSavage.

> **Honestly just should've improved on not getting sniped and getting bugged. All my fault ofc, wish I was as good as everyone top 10 that knew how to not get bugged and sniped.**
>
> *Martin*

Anne: 'In the solos, Benjy was aiming for top 10, however he got sniped in two of the games and instantly finished. In his last game, he started falling off a ramp and was sniped down. Benjy ended up positioning in 25th place. As parents, Johnny and I found it best to not talk with the boys more than necessary, both before and after entering the stage. Benjy and Martin are both top athletes in their field and they independently know how they performed and what they need to focus on.'

Johnny: 'Martin finished in 29th position in the solos competition. I remember when he was speaking about his tournament experience; he said that he found the duo finals had been surprisingly laggy, probably due to all the world best professional players playing in the same game. Martin believed he played well but he knew there was room for improvement.'

> **Nothing better than eating a juicy pizza and watching some Minecraft after missing top 10.**
>
> *Martin*

Martin and Turner "Tfue" Tenney watching Benjy during the solo finals. Photo credit @joetidy.

WORLD CUP AFTERMATH

Johnny: 'It is fair to say that both boys were devastated that they hadn't done as well in the World Cup as they wanted to. They knew that they had the potential to be as good as anyone else taking part. All parents can do is try to be there for their children when they need support, as well as giving them space when they need it. Having a good peer and support team around them is also important. The day after the tournament, Martin relaxed at the hotel room and went sightseeing in New York City, visiting the Empire State Building and then Fifth Avenue for some shopping. Later that evening, Martin went back to the Helix eSports Center to resume practice, determined to do better in the next event.'

Anne: 'After the finals, Benjy decided to go out with his friends and wind down from the weekend's events. Despite the disappointment one of the most memorable moments during the event for Benjy was the iconic "thumbs-up" he gave to the camera at the stadium. At the time, it was great to see him starting to relax and enjoy the experience.

Benjy and Martin, as professional players, have both come out stronger from their World Cup experience with more drive, intensity, and focus. They know what to expect from the next competition and have taken the disappointment and channelled it into moving forward. This is the sign of any good professional player in any sport or discipline.'

> **Honestly one of the best moments of my life and it's me putting my thumbs up.**
>
> *Benjy*

At Times Square, New York City. From left to right: Noward, Chibi, Benjy, Fuji, Smeef, Svennoss. Photo credit benjyfishy.

MENTAL ATTITUDE

The main focus of professional athletes of all fields, including esports, is winning and striving to be the best. Benjy and Martin are both driven by their aspirations to achieve victory.

Motivation is difficult to sustain as it involves tough challenges and sacrifices. Players require a strong support network behind them, including their parents, to help them achieve their goals.

MENTAL ATTITUDE

In a similar way to the start of most sporting careers, gaming usually begins with a player casually gaming with friends; they discover their talent and decide to take it to a competitive level. But competing is not the same as playing. Professional Fortnite requires mental focus, determination and hard work, comparable to top athletes in traditional sports.

DESIRE AND HARD WORK

Benjy and Martin have always had a strong and unfaltering desire to win, which makes it easier for them to set clear goals. They prioritise their careers and will always ask themselves if an action or decision will improve their competitive results; if not it is less likely that they will go ahead. Many sponsorships and interviews have been turned down due to this.

The secret behind success is hard work, but keep in mind that hard work is not just about putting in the hours grinding. It involves being disciplined and maintaining a balance between your gaming activities, like scrims, tournaments, VOD reviews, alongside life activities like sleeping a healthy amount, getting the right nutrition and spending time with family and friends.

Losing and having a bad game are inevitable, however being resilient and not giving up is a skill, which can be practised and mastered.

Successful players know how to move on after a bad game and direct their energy into playing better in future games. Sometimes both Benjy and Martin bang their desks to vent their frustration. The loud noise might be worrying for a parent to hear, however it can be an important way for the players to express their disappointment and reset their mental state to get ready for the next game.

In the World Cup Finals in New York 2019, Benjy gave a shout-out to Mongraal.

> " ngl shoutout to Mongraal, he was on 0 points the first 2/3 games then popped off in the last games, and big congrats to Bugha. "
>
> *Benjy*

CONSTANT IN-GAME CHANGES

Traditional sports stay fairly consistent in their rules, however this is not the case for Fortnite, where the game is constantly changing. For example, every three to four months an overhauled map is introduced and each week there is a smaller update, which often requires the players to learn new skills and adjust their gameplay. This demands that players are alert and adaptable to change.

One of the key factors in Fortnite is where to land on the map, this landing spot is something that the players practise and perfect for weeks.

ESL KATOWICE ROYALE

In 2019, the ESL Katowice Royale tournament in Poland took place, however in less than 24 hours before the start of the event, the new Fortnite Season 8 launched. The whole North Eastern side of the map changed and some of the landing spots had been completely wiped out, giving players very little time to adjust to the new updates.

> " I'm at 3 day $500k tournament and I'm ready! Oh wait my drop spot just got removed. "
>
> *Poach*

Martin on nervousness during his Mental State AdvanceClass, October 2020:

" Nervousness before tournaments isn't necessarily a bad thing. Nervousness gets you more focused. Tell yourself that you have prepared for this. You have practised as much as you can and there is nothing more you could have done. Also, breathe really slowly in and out. Even in a 1v1 situation – it will help you gain confidence and clear your head. If you're angry tell yourself to focus on the game and the tasks ahead. "

Martin

TEAM CHANGES

Players often switch teams in Fortnite, which can often cause conflicts between friend groups. In these situations, it is important to treat other players with respect and part ways on as good terms as possible. Benjy would not have switched trios in 2019 if Martin had not agreed to it (see page 128).

COMMITMENT

It is clear from reading this book that professional players have to make sacrifices to commit to a career in esports. It is a full-time job, which demands that a player performs at their best and keeps up with their competitors. This means a player's education may be disrupted and that they may have to limit the amount of time they spend on their other interests and activities outside gaming.

Players may have to change their diets, follow an exercise plan and make sure they stick to a good sleep pattern. This might put a lot of young people off professional gaming, however it is important to seriously consider what kinds of commitments are involved in maintaining a career in esports.

" Don't blame things on bad luck. Instead practise mental resets and focus on your goals. "

Martin

Photo credit 100 Thieves.

TIPS FOR PARENTS

1 Familiarise yourself more with Fortnite. If you search 'Fortnite for parents' on YouTube, you will find informative videos for the complete novice. Even some basic knowledge is better than nothing.

2 Your child probably has higher expectations of esports than you do. Do not push your child but build the support network they need to enable them to achieve their best.

3 Support their dreams within reason. Give them a certain amount of freedom and responsibility of managing their gaming, which will allow them to grow and mature.

4 If your child becomes a professional player, let them own the process it took to achieve their goal. Avoid micro managing and interfering too much with their achievements.

5 If your child starts earning a lot of money, be sensitive not to rely on them to financially support your household. It is a heavy burden to put on a young person and they should have the freedom to quit playing at any time.

6 Celebrate your child's achievement and let them know that you are proud of them. They will benefit from this love and support, even though they may not acknowledge it.

7 Don't try to handle defeats for them, just simply be present or close by if they need you. At LANs, provide them with some food and drink and be prepared to leave them alone if they need their own space.

8 Cheating is known to occur in esports, especially in online play when organisers cannot check players' equipment. We encourage you to take a clear stance against it. Likewise, support your child if they become a victim of cheating.

TIPS FOR PLAYERS

1 Divide your big goals into smaller ones and reward yourself for the small goals when you reach them. This makes it easier not to give up.

2 Plan how you are going to handle the times when things go wrong. If you have the right attitude, over time you can turn anything around.

3 If you have been feeling tired and de-motivated for more than two weeks, treat that as a signal for change and consider what is out of balance.

4 Don't forget your teammates while chasing your goals. Set goals in building good and long-lasting relationships with your teammates.

5 Speak to your parents about your gaming goals.

> **If people say I am washed then it drives me to be better.**
>
> *Benjy*

Martin's "MRSAVAGE" logo with the characteristic "skull S" referring back to his usage of the purple Skull Trooper skin in Fortnite. © MrSavage.

Martin focused during the DreamHack Anaheim Fortnite finals, February 2020. Photo credit 100 Thieves.

The collective gathering of players nurtures a strong community spirit. Martin always looks forward to meeting other players IRL. Photo from DreamHack Anaheim in 2020. From left to right: Shayan "ShyoWager" Shehryar, Diego "Arkhram" Lima, Martin, Brendan "Falconer" Falconer, Brodie "Rehx" Franks and Arten "Ballatw" Esa. Photo credit 100 Thieves.

STAYING AT THE TOP

Competitive gaming involves a lot of dedication and hard work over a long period. Staying at the top equally involves hard and sustained dedication and is, in some respects, even harder than fulfilling the primary goal.

" When they start earning lots of money from streaming or gaining followers etc they start getting side tracked and forget about what first got them into it, which is wanting to be the best, and that's how pro players end up becoming washed or uninterested with the game. If you want to stay at the top, you need to always be wanting to be the best. "

Benjy

Getting a lot of followers and public attention ultimately means that a player will also be exposed to a lot of varied comments and viewpoints from an unbelievably vast number of people. If you are streaming and have a social media presence it is impossible to avoid all that attention which may be difficult to handle mentally.

A WASHED PLAYER

Some online attention can be negative, with players becoming the subject of criticism and negativity. Players can be unfairly labelled as washed up or irrelevant, if they haven't won any big competitions lately, often ignoring their actual results and performance. This is what happened to Martin during the fall of 2019.

" After trios [FNCS] was finished, people were like already starting to call me washed because … um … I didn't even do really bad in trios; we just didn't have any pop-offs. In trios, I placed like 15th average in the FNCS qualifiers and then the finals I placed 7th. "

Martin

THE MRSAVAGE EFFECT

Leven2k, a Fortnite caster, coined the term "The MrSavage Effect" in a podcast, on his YouTube channel, in May 2020: 'The Savage Effect is where a player becomes a lot less visible in the public eye and therefore the casual fan is less able to see their ability and to see that they're still performing. As a lot of the time fans are too lazy to actually check where players are performing and placing.'

Leven2k, the professional commentator and analyst who coined "The MrSavage effect" term. Photo credit @Leven2k.

" I don't consider myself washed.

All the Tweets of me saying for example «washed player makes a comeback» is just to make fun of people who genuinely think so. "

Martin

TURN NEGATIVITY INTO MOTIVATION

In Martin's case this actually led to a downward spiral, he stopped streaming for a few months and as a result he became even less visible. But there was a reason behind his actions that Martin explains in his own words: 'After everyone started calling me like washed and stuff, I kind of stopped streaming to focus more on competitive stuff because I really wanted to prove people wrong.'

Martin was able to turn the negativity into the motivation to become a better player. This paid off, because just a couple of months later he was again considered one of the best players in the world.

PROVING THEM WRONG

It is very easy to criticise others but it can be very difficult to receive criticism. Martin decided to view this as an opportunity for improvement and growth as a player.

This is how Leven2k sums it up in his podcast: 'Right now people see MrSavage as one of the best players in the world, easily. Well, to put it simply, he won DreamHack and in quite an amazing fashion to say the least. Not only did he win DreamHack, though. He also signed to 100 Thieves. He started streaming a lot more. He started uploading a lot more content to YouTube and in general his social media presence became a lot more visible. Now this is a cycle that I like to call the MrSavage Effect named after him, because I think he's the most famous example of it.'

Needless to say Martin's "washed" period was tough on him. In his AdvanceClass on Mental State he says: 'A lot of players would probably just stop playing the game or at least play it less because they weren't getting the support they were before.'

Johnny: 'After Martin won DreamHack Anaheim, there was an enormous feeling of joy to see him come out on top, but it was also filled with relief after seeing the end of a challenging period.'

Martin at DreamHack Anaheim 2020.
Photo credit 100 Thieves.

BENJY HANDLING PRESSURE - HOW IT STARTED VS HOW IT IS GOING

Anne: 'Benjy never saw his age as a barrier to success and often competed with children a lot older than him, including his brother Charles. Every Saturday morning I would take them along to the local ten-pin bowling club. Benjy would go along to spectate and watch the weekly league matches. He was captivated and it wasn't long before he was insisting that he wanted to play as well.

On Benjy's 2nd birthday he finally got his wish. He managed to push a bowling ball down the lane for the first time, by using a ramp, and was instantly hooked. Remarkably within the year he had managed to develop a double-handed technique to throw the ball down the lane, without the aid of any bumper rails and started knocking down the pins. This was the stepping-stone he needed to start taking part in some tournaments.'

BOWLING TOURNAMENTS

Anne: 'Benjy participated in his first bowling competition at the 2008 South of England, Junior Open Tournament in Dunstable. On the day of the tournament I remember Benjy being very overwhelmed by his new surroundings, as he had never been to the centre before.

When it was time for him to throw his first ball, Benjy's nerves got the better of him and he tripped on a small step on the approach, which he was not used to when playing on a Saturday at Guildford Youth Bowling Club (YBC). As a result he got very upset, but the coaches calmed him down and he managed to continue playing and score some points. He even left with a trophy. Awarded to him for being the youngest player at the competition.

That experience taught Benjy that in competitions, if you fall down, you have to pick yourself straight up again and carry on.'

UNDERSTANDING LANE CONDITIONS

Playing competitive ten-pin bowling is not simply just a case of throwing a ball down the lane – it is highly skilled. The lanes have different oil patterns on them and it is important to know what type of ball to use, where to stand and what to do when the lanes start 'drying out'.

Anne: 'When Benjy was taking part in the tournaments especially at a young age, he would find it difficult to master these bowling techniques. Sometimes when the lane was drying out it meant that if he slightly moved position it could be the difference between getting a strike or a gutter ball. As a result, there have been several events where Benjy has 'gone to pieces' because a game or tournament didn't go well and was unable to pull himself mentally back to perform well. In these scenarios Benjy often doubted his skills, however it was simply a case that he hadn't understood the lane conditions.

Benjy went on to have success in bowling tournaments with his ultimate goal to play for England. Unfortunately, due to developing Osgood-Schlatter's he was in a lot of pain while bowling and had to stop which is how he came to be playing Fortnite and took the competitive drive that he had in traditional sport over to esports.'

Benjy aged 4 with his bowling trophy. Photo credit Anne Fish.

FAST FORWARD TO FORTNITE

Over the years Benjy has learnt how to handle pressure and to master his mental attitude when it matters most, even when tournaments have not started out that well in the beginning. Never give up as tournaments are won or lost quite often in the last match. Both Benjy and Martin have mastered the ability to handle pressure when competitions are not going well.

> **Holy shit man, I came back so hard, was 50th place after game 4, then after game 4 i had loading screen bug, i reset my mental and popped off the last 3 games, finished 11th ($6.25k) ggs.**
>
> *Benjy*

> *I was solo herettic dc'd and i got like 15 kills solo endgame and won holy there is no wayyyyyyyyy.*

DAILY DUOS CUP

EUROPE OPEN

#1	**Heretticc & NRGbenjyfishy**	**185**
#2	**100T MrSavage & MSF Endretta**	**182**

COACHES AND ANALYSTS

Fortnite Battle Royale was released in September 2017, which has not allowed much time for esports coaches and analysts to develop their professional role, supporting professional players.

Due to the individualistic nature of Fortnite, with solo players and teams forming across esports organisations, there appears to be a reluctance from organisations to invest in this kind of professional support. This is however changing, as current Fortnite professional players have started looking for new career opportunities.

The role of an esports coach has been established for years within other multi-player games such as Overwatch, CS:GO and League of Legends. Erik "Bloodx" Guttormsen was perhaps one of the first players to enter such a role within Fortnite. Bloodx played a crucial part as Martin's duo partner and mentor during Martin's breakthrough in late 2018. In February 2021 Bloodx became Fortnite Head Coach at the esports organisation Apeks (see interview at page 112). During the lead-up to the Fortnite World Cup in 2019, professional player Hugh "DestinysJesus" Gilmour spent time analysing landing spots and background information. Subsequently he went on to join the esports organisation FaZe Clan to develop his career as a coach under the name FaZe Destiny (see interview at page 116).

Players are also starting to coach their peers during big tournaments. At the NA East Bugha Throwback Cup, in July 2020, FaZe Mark "Bizzle" Felder coached NRG Cody "Clix" Conrod live on stream which lead to his victory. Benjy and Martin have also supported other players: in May 2020, during the FNCS Solo Invitational they coached Turner "Tfue" Tenney.

Coach analysis of videos and gameplay (VOD reviews) on YouTube also plays a vital role in helping aspiring players improve their game.

Both Benjy and Martin are part of various groups on Discord (see page 188) where elite players help each other improve, but also coaches and mentors like Bloodx and DestinysJesus participate.

Benjy and Martin have not yet hired a coach on a permanent basis, but that may change in the future.

WHAT IS AN ESPORTS COACH?

Tom Dore, the Head of Education at the British Esports Association, explains it like this:

'Like traditional sports, a coach will help the team train against other teams (aka 'scrim') in order to improve.

Coaches work closely with the players, to motivate them, identify their strengths and weaknesses and make sure they are playing at their best. They will develop strategies and analyse opponents in order to win as many matches – and tournaments – as possible.

A coach is responsible for every aspect relating to performance within a team. This includes, but is not limited to, growth of individual skill of the players, team cohesion, in-game strategy, motivational responsibilities and discipline.'

WHAT IS AN ESPORTS ANALYST?

Tom Dore explains it like this:

'Analysts are experts at taking information and using it to provide interesting stats or learn from it, either for a particular team, tournament provider, broadcaster or game developer.

Team analysts usually work with coaches to generate strategies, analyse strengths and weaknesses, and communicate this to the players in order to get the best out of them. Sometimes a person will be responsible for both coaching and analyst duties.

Some companies or developers will employ analysts or statisticians to keep track of facts, stats and other game information throughout each season.'

Among professional Fortnite players the terms "coach" and "analyst" seem to be used interchangeably, with more use of the former than the latter.

Rocket League coach and British Esports game adviser, Mike 'Gregan' Ellis, supporting one of his players. Photo credit Joe Brady, Gfinity.

ERIK "BLOODX" GUTTORMSEN

Esports mentor and Fortnite head coach at Apeks, a Norwegian esports organisation

Bloodx acts as a mentor and coach for the professional EU Fortnite players IDrop and Krizzii at Apeks, and TaySon at Falcon. Bloodx played a key role as Martin's mentor during his breakthrough in late 2018. He takes a direct approach and is not afraid of challenging his elite players.

 ### WHAT BROUGHT YOU TO THE POSITION YOU HAVE TODAY?

Bloodx: 'I've always been extremely competitive and grew up playing football, FIFA and a lot of World of Warcraft (WoW). I was top ranked in Europe in WoW during my teenage years but my parents didn't allow me to play competitions, so I empathise with any young players in the same situation. When Fortnite launched in 2017 I fell in love with the game. I was probably among the first professional players to work hard at the game from a deep strategic perspective.'

 ### HOW DO YOU SELECT THE PLAYERS YOU WORK WITH?

Bloodx: 'I say no to most requests from players as I only want to work with the best EU pro players — what I call elite pro players. These players have the winning mentality necessary to progress on a steady learning curve, and they really want to put in the hours to get to the top level. Since EU is the largest Fortnite region, there is likely that these players are at a top level globally.'

 ### HOW DID YOU MEET MARTIN?

Bloodx: 'I saw Martin in July 2018 when he was streaming solo custom games (invite only games often used for competitive practice) and I instantly noticed his mechanical skills. We started chatting on Discord and I was delighted when I found out that he also was Norwegian. A week later he won a Solo Showdown tournament (a limited time game mode) and we eventually decided to play duos together. Playing duos with him gave me the opportunity to teach him the importance of strategical out-of-the-box thinking.'

 ### WHAT CHARACTERISES AN ELITE PLAYER?

Bloodx: 'They are extremely intuitive in how they approach situations, and are fast and keen learners. They quickly get to the core of problems as they have the ability to correct things proactively, when most other players don't even realize that they are about to run into a problem in-game. They have a good memory of past situations, they think and react fast which is necessary to analyse all options in complex surroundings.'

Q HOW DO YOU WORK WITH PLAYERS AT THAT LEVEL?

Bloodx: 'I start out with establishing a clear structure of how to play the game and a routine for the player to strictly follow until they master it. This is needed to avoid wasting time on unnecessary considerations during a game. After all, Fortnite is among the fastest paced games there is. A prerequisite is that the player is ready and has faith in my process and abilities. There is a difference between asking for help and being ready for help.'

Q AND HOW DO YOU BUILD ON THIS FOUNDATION AS A COACH?

Bloodx: 'When the players master the routine and structure, they can start making it their own. Fortnite players are exposed to an unimaginable high number of different scenarios in-game. The way I approach this is to help players to learn not only by analysing past games, but to learn how to foresee as much as possible while in-game. It is perhaps this ability that makes TaySon and MrSavage among the best players in the world.'

Q HOW DO YOU TEACH PLAYERS THIS?

Bloodx: 'I need to work with players one-on-one and spend a lot of time with each one of them to adjust their gameplay. And not only in hours but also over time periods of months and preferably years. This is why I can't work with more than a few players at a time. I don't spend time on what players can do themselves — they need to learn by doing, even the simplest of tasks.'

Bloodx in his Apeks jersey.
Photo credit BetongFilm.

THE MEDIA SOMETIMES PRESENT ELITE PLAYERS IN TRADITIONAL SPORTS AS ARROGANT INDIVIDUALS WHO THINK THEY KNOW IT ALL. IS THAT THE SAME IN FORTNITE?

Bloodx: 'Elite players are of course strong headed with a winner mentality and not afraid of sharing their opinion. But you will not get to the absolute top if you don't listen to criticism. I'm a straight talker and I tell them exactly what I think they do wrong and what they need to improve. I focus on their weaknesses, which are mostly in-game qualities but also things outside the game. I think it is essential that these players meet some pushback on their weak sides. This sometimes develops into heated debates but it is these situations, more often than not, when the real progress takes place. Don't get me wrong, of course I support my players, but on an elite level the focus is different. One needs to challenge the players in various creative ways to bring out the best in them. In doing this one feels manipulative and crazy at times – but I strongly think this is needed. It is all about winning and not being carried by a well-meaning friend.'

 HOW INTENSE DO THE 'HEATED DEBATES' GET?

Bloodx: 'Quite intense at times! That's why we put some distance between us once in a while – both in time and space. Now and then it gets to the point that we are so fed up with each other that we don't speak for days and even weeks.'

 DO YOU DECIDE YOUR PLAYERS' PLAYSTYLE?

Bloodx: 'I challenge them with my views, which makes them re-evaluate and improve their own playstyle. A players' style is an expression of their innate qualities and I don't want to take that away from them. I just want to improve on their weaknesses and make them the best version of themselves - capable of learning and winning consistently – as a solo or a trio, or in whatever game mode.'

 DO YOU ALSO ADVISE ON PLAYERS OUT-OF-GAME ROUTINES SUCH AS NUTRITION, SLEEP ETC?

Bloodx: 'Fortnite has only been around for a few years and I think as the competitive environment matures we will see the importance of these aspects increase. Fortnite tournaments typically last for nearly 3.5 hours and you sometimes play two of them in one day. It goes without saying that a top player needs to work out physically, get enough regular sleep and eat properly.'

 DOES THE YOUNG AGE OF FORTNITE PLAYERS POSE A PROBLEM?

Bloodx: 'I'm tempted to answer a straight yes. It is of course a question of maturity. You can't expect players at thirteen years of age to be mature. But what you can expect is to be treated with respect as a mentor and coach, and through this give the young players enough leeway to mature over time. But it feels like parenting at times, where participants in discussion groups don't respect and appreciate my experience and results. Hopefully books like this can increase awareness and make players and parents aware of what it takes to compete and win.'

Martin meeting Bloodx for the first time IRL in Trondheim, Norway, in December 2018. Photo credit Johnny Troset Andersen.

WHAT IS THE DIFFERENCE BETWEEN A MENTOR AND A COACH?

Bloodx: 'In my opinion coaching is about guidance toward clear goals, while mentoring is about sharing a wider range of skills and experience. Mentoring is more long term and I would love for my players to be able to pass it on to the next generation of players.'

> **Bloodx opened up my eyes to the creative and strategical side of Fortnite and he was essential in helping me reach some of my potential.**
>
> *Martin*

WHAT WOULD YOUR ADVICE BE TO YOUNG ASPIRING FORTNITE COACHES?

Bloodx: 'I've seen some Fortnite coaches that simply don't know their game well enough. I think it is a clear advantage to have played and studied the game for thousands of hours. Since the game is still quite new, there isn't many well-structured courses and textbooks yet. I think a coach needs to have played on a high pro level to make a significant difference for their players.'

ANY ADVICE FOR ASPIRING PRO PLAYERS?

Bloodx: 'You need to be quite tough with yourself to win. At some point not everything is fun anymore – you need to set goals and be honest with yourself. Take a look around – there are few that actually succeed as top athletes in any sports and even fewer that are able to stay at the top over time. But the most important thing is to be curious and keep learning; otherwise you will be surpassed quickly. You can't have a negative attitude towards learning and a key part of learning is to listen and reflect on what you learn.'

HUGH "DESTINYSJESUS" GILMOUR

Former Fortnite coach for FaZe Clan

A coach is an invaluable resource to improve your gameplay but it is not often affordable, so esports organisations sometimes employ coaches for their players. DestinysJesus is a coach who produces educational videos. We interviewed him while he still worked for the esports organisation FaZe Clan.

Q COULD YOU TELL US ABOUT YOUR BACKGROUND AND HOW YOU ENDED UP AS A FORTNITE COACH?

DestinysJesus: 'I worked at a gym doing one-to-one coaching when I was about 16–17 years old. Most people I worked with were younger than me. I also did powerlift coaching and competing. I started playing Fortnite competitively when it was released and I participated in all the weeks leading up to the 2019 Fortnite World Cup, but didn't qualify. I learned a lot and with my background in one-to-one work it felt natural for me to transition into coaching qualified players for the World Cup finals.'

Q HOW DID YOU END UP WORKING WITH BENJY AND MARTIN IN THE LEAD-UP TO THE WORLD CUP 2019?

DestinysJesus: 'Benjy was actually the first one I worked with and since Benjy and Martin were duos, it became natural to work with Martin also. After that a lot of other people and organisations were interested and messaged me. The 2019 Fortnite World Cup was a huge event and there was only four or five Fortnite coaches at that time. The demand was high, and I did a lot of freelance work at that time. I worked with the top three players in both the solos and duos finals, and several others.'

Q HOW WOULD YOU CHARACTERISE BENJY AND MARTIN AS PLAYERS?

DestinysJesus: 'Compared to other pro Fortnite players, I think they are the most adaptable to whatever changes Epic Games decides to do to the game, like pumps vaulted or bouncer traps added. When a new season comes out, they are one of the top duo teams instantly, while other players need more time to adjust to the new meta.'

Q DID YOU GO TO NEW YORK FOR THE WORLD CUP IN 2019?

DestinysJesus: 'No, but I would have loved that, of course. I had puppies at the time, so I had to prioritise.'

Q HOW DID YOU GET SIGNED AS A COACH FOR FAZE CLAN?

DestinysJesus: 'After the 2019 World Cup Finals a lot of organisations were interested in getting me to exclusively work on their pro players. However, I ended up working non-exclusively for several orgs during a couple of FNCS Tournaments, but FaZe players did quite well during these, so I ended up accepting an offer from FaZe. Now I work exclusively for FaZe as a coach on the 1:1 pro player level, but I'm allowed to publish my own courses for other players and do content on my own.'

DestinysJesus at his desk at home.
Photo credit Emily Mudie Photography.

Q ARE YOU RESPONSIBLE FOR COACHING ALL FAZE'S FORTNITE PLAYERS?

DestinysJesus: 'The majority of the FaZe guys I work with are NA East, but I'm obviously focused on the EU because I compete in the EU and I work with Mongraal. I coach in all game modes, i.e. solos, duos, trios and squads.'

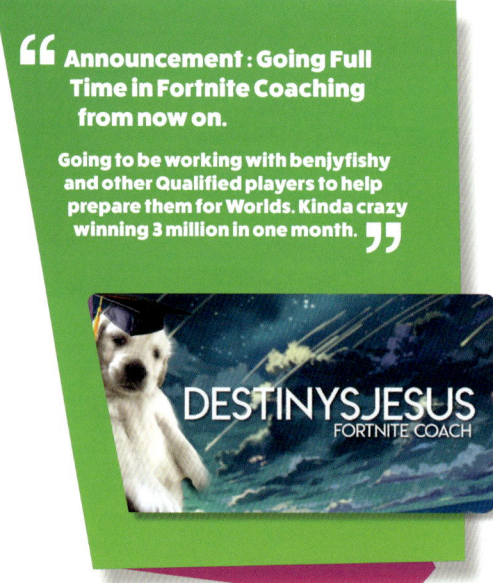

" **Announcement : Going Full Time in Fortnite Coaching from now on.**

Going to be working with benjyfishy and other Qualified players to help prepare them for Worlds. Kinda crazy winning 3 million in one month. "

DESTINYSJESUS
FORTNITE COACH

Q WHAT TYPE OF FORTNITE COACHING SERVICES DO YOU PROVIDE?

DestinysJesus: 'Besides one-to-one coaching, I decided to make online courses to reach out to more players. My solo classes consist of almost 40 videos and there are also almost 20 videos of my box fighting classes. The classes are aimed at all players from beginners to pros.'

Q WHAT TYPE OF IN-GAME SKILLS DO YOU THINK ARE MOST IMPORTANT FOR A PLAYER?

DestinysJesus: 'It is without a doubt being smart – having the right 'game sense'- that is knowing what to do in certain situations like knowing how to rotate. The whole concept of Fortnite is just to have the best end game possible, and you have to be really smart up to that point and make sure everything is perfect. To achieve this you need to understand the game at a really deep level.'

Q WHAT ADVICE WOULD YOU GIVE AN ASPIRING PROFESSIONAL PLAYER WHO HASN'T MADE IT TO THE TOP YET?

DestinysJesus: 'Every player at the top level is really good mechanically with a good aim. But the difference between the top 5 and top 50 is their knowledge of the game. You can win a game and think all you did was perfect, but technically it may not be the right play because you got lucky. Your instincts may be wrong, so you really need to put your effort into reviewing your gameplay by VOD, reviewing yourself or with the help of friends or a coach.'

Q WHAT ADVICE WOULD YOU GIVE A COMPLETE BEGINNER TO IMPROVE THEIR GAMEPLAY?

DestinysJesus: 'If you are very new to the game you should enter into Fortnite's creative mode and practise your mechanical skills, which naturally involve getting to know the keybinds and training your muscle memory. Then start playing real games and consistently VOD reviewing as soon as possible.

Write notes and make a plan for what to work on. You would also benefit from watching others' VOD reviews, or do VOD reviews of other players yourself. Remember to VOD review from an opponent's point-of-view, not only your own point-of-view.'

Q DO YOU HAVE ANY ADVICE FOR PARENTS OF FORTNITE PLAYERS?

DestinysJesus: 'Help your child keep to a good schedule around Fortnite that takes into account warm-ups, tournaments and practice, and balances it with a consistent sleep schedule, family time and schoolwork. It is difficult, but that is exactly why parents should be involved to help. Be aware that the Fortnite tournament schedule is hard to plan around, as it is set for short calendar periods and time of days, and sometimes arranged as late as a few days before. There is no year-long calendar in Fortnite, which would have been really nice. And scrims – which is pro practice that pro players organise in-between themselves – sometimes come with just a few hours' or even minutes' warning.'

For more information about DestinysJesus' Fortnite coaching services visit: www.destinysjesus.com

DestinysJesus and Poppy. Photo credit Emily Mudie Photography.

INTERVIEW WITH
FALCON ALWYZPAPPIE

Christof Vanderlinden, otherwise known as Falcon AlwyzPAPPIE, is a mental coach for Falcon esports, supporting the mental health of professional Fortnite players

Before he discovered Fortnite, Christof was a self-confessed workaholic running three companies simultaneously. In 2019, he was was given the suspected diagnosis of neuromuscular disease (MS) which left him in a wheelchair. His doctors are still not completely sure how to diagnose his condition. Confined to his home, his children introduced him to Fortnite, which soon became his new passion. Christof now shares his story to support and inspire others. He works as a mental coach for Falcon esports and is an advisor at COPE (see page 218).

 HOW DID YOUR MS DIAGNOSIS CHANGE YOUR LIFE?

Christof: 'In the beginning people thought I was just burnt out, as my body just stopped working properly. Because I was in a wheelchair people would ask if I was OK or needed to be pushed, and I found that hard to deal with. I still have to ask my kids to open my water bottles, since I don't have the strength in my hands. My diagnosis changed everything, but it didn't change me. It didn't change my drive, it didn't change my personality; it only shifted things towards new goals and new heights.'

 HOW DID YOU DISCOVER FORTNITE AND DID YOU HAVE A BACKGROUND IN GAMING?

Christof: 'It was my oldest son who begged to play Fortnite. We were the parents that thought shooting games would be bad, but after some research into it we allowed him to start playing. He hated the challenges but loved the game itself. When I finished working, in the early hours of the morning, I would start to learn the mechanics and do the challenges for him, so at least he would have all the skins. But it was when I got sick that I downloaded Fortnite on my Macbook and fell in love with the game.'

 HOW DID YOUR HEALTH CONDITION AFFECT YOUR GAMING?

Christof: 'When I didn't have the strength to grip the controller anymore, I decided to try KBM (keyboard and mouse) but this hurt my hands even more. One of my doctors, who games with his son, told me that because of the building aspect in Fortnite I wouldn't be able to play it anymore. This was exactly what I needed: somebody to prove wrong! I then discovered the Azeron, which is a 3D printed keypad that wraps around your hand so that you can comfortably reach the buttons. I worked closely with the manufacturer, as their main focus is to take care of gamers just like me.'

 WHICH PROFESSIONAL FORTNITE PLAYERS INSPIRED YOU?

Christof: 'Bugha has played a huge role in what I do. I was pretty down one night because I didn't have control of my hand, it just didn't want to work and moved on its own all the time. I hadn't been able to game for days and my progress was declining. One evening I was watching Bugha's stream and he was trying to play an event with new keybinds. He was stressed but he kept going despite the unsupportive comments of the majority of his viewers. I was amazed by his strength and perseverance.'

Photo credit AlwyzPAPPIE.

HOW DID YOU BECOME A MENTAL COACH FOR FALCON ESPORTS?

Christof: 'I started to work with some mid-tier players with positive results. Slowly more and more people needed advice. I then started to coach the top players mentally as well as on a performance and team level. I had a good success rate in coaching. I helped Rezon recover after his huge dip after not qualifying for DreamHack. In March 2021, I put Hen, Chapix and JannisZ together as a team two days before the FNCS. I coached them through video messages, where I would use specific language to get them into the right mental state. They went on to dominate that FNCS.

I also coached Jur3ky, Queasy and TruleX who eventually won the FNCS Trios in May 2021. After that, Team Falcon reached out, I also had some other offers from T1 orgs but they didn't fit my mission, vision and goals. I felt that Team Falcon was very family-oriented, an organisation where you all strive to be one, and that made my decision easy.'

WHAT DOES A JOB AS AN ESPORTS MENTAL COACH INVOLVE?

Christof: 'I analyse the players and their personalities, and recommend specific routines and exercises to suit them. I want my players to be the best version of themselves not only in the game but also outside of the game, making sure they are healthy and happy. I have to prepare them mentally for an ultimate performance, but also when things don't go as planned so they can bounce back. Also I have to make sure the top players don't get bored and are able to transfer their passion for other goals outside of gaming back into gaming so they stay at their best. For trios, I work with them on a team level so they understand each other, improve their communication and work as one team for the same goal.'

WHAT OTHER ESPORTS COACHES INSPIRE YOU?

Christof: 'DestinysJesus is an amazing coach. He added me in group sessions with some of the T2 and T3 players, and that's where I discovered my strengths and passion. I have also been duo coaching with both Bloodx and BL Sven. But I will never forget a coaching session where Vadeal and I coached Karma for the FNCS Allstars. Vadeal was so accurate and to the point. He is an example of the future potential for professional players after they decide to stop playing the game.'

TELL US ABOUT YOUR WORK FOR COPE (COALITION OF PARENTS IN ESPORTS)?

Christof: '#togetherwecope is exactly what I stand for, as together we COPE to make this scene a better place. Although I'm not a parent of a pro player, I see my players as my other kids and I also work closely with their parents. It's my goal to spread more awareness about COPE and everything they do in the background. I love the team and the weekly meetings we have and I'm always amazed how hard they work in the background.'

TELL US ABOUT HOW YOU GOT IN TOUCH WITH ANNE "MAMABENJYFISHY" FISH AND YOUR DUO PARTNERSHIP?

Christof: 'Anne is a positive spark in the scene. I love how she works to help and guide the new generation based on her own experience with Benjy. I watched her making her first steps in the game as a player and then starting to play at a higher level. We then connected through our work at COPE and decided to play some games and events together in the most fun way. Anne is inspirational and the younger generation look up to her, and I'm proud to call her a friend.'

Q WHAT IS YOUR KEY ADVICE TO ASPIRING FORTNITE PLAYERS WHO HAVE LONG-TERM HEALTH CONDITIONS OR DISABILITIES?

Christof: 'There are so many possibilities to play at a high level. The conditions might be super hard but when you have a positive mindset you can overcome everything. Investigate how you can adapt, push and have fun, because a disability will never stop you from chasing your dream. Think of solutions instead of problems and you are not alone. For example, Permastunned is an amazing esports team and group of people that will always be there to help you and overcome your problems.'

Q WHAT ARE YOUR AMBITIONS AND GOALS FOR YOUR FUTURE IN ESPORTS?

Christof: 'My goal is to create a legacy with AlwyzPAPPIE. My mission and vision are to change this scene one step at a time. I want to highlight the importance of mental coaching so that players are not pushing themselves to the limit every day, as burnout is a common thing. I want to make the scene less toxic and more supportive overall, so it becomes a positive place where everybody can develop. I know I will not be super long in this scene because of my illness, but I want to make the absolute best of it. No matter how hard life hits you, you can achieve absolute greatness, and no matter how hard you fall just get up and create a positive mindset.'

The 3D printed keypad from Azeron that Christof uses. Photo credit AlwyzPAPPIE.

BOOTCAMPS & LAN TOURNAMENTS

The worldwide attraction of esports gives players a unique opportunity to find out about different countries and cultures, as well as to make life-long friends from places that they might not ordinarily be exposed to.

International bootcamps and LAN tournaments play an important role for players, as they offer an opportunity to meet each other in real life.

The stage at the Australian Open (AO) Summer Smash 2020. Benjy participated in the Charity Pro-Am Trio event and the solo event. Photo credit Tennis Australia.

PROAM PRIZE POOL	
1ST	$30,000
2ND	$21,000
3RD	$15,000
4TH	$12,000
5TH	$6,000
6TH	$4,500
7-10TH	$3,000
TOTAL	$100,000

PROAM PRIZE POOL	
1ST	$30,000
2ND	$21,000
3RD	$15,000
4TH	$12,000
5TH	$6,000
6TH	$4,500
7-10TH	$3,000
TOTAL	$100,000

In the lead-up to the 2019 World Cup, Benjy visited Fnatic's headquarters in London during the qualifying weekends. It was here that Benjy got to meet Kyle "Mongraal" Jackson for the first time. In addition, he was able to spend time at the Cooler esports house, which also was in London.

FRANKFURT BOOTCAMP

Anne: 'From my experience as a parent of a Fortnite professional, you find out very quickly that tournaments can be announced with little warning and subsequently you have to adjust your schedule to suit this. I remember having to adapt to various changes during the events surrounding the announcement of the Trios Season X FNCS Tournament in 2019.

Benjy teamed up with Kyle "Mongraal" Jackson and Dmitri "Mitr0" Van de Vrie (abbreviated to MMB by fans of the trio) and he announced that they would be going to a bootcamp in Frankfurt, Germany, for a month. There was then a mad panic, liaising with everyone to get the logistics planned as well as organising who would be able to chaperone the players during the trip.'

Kylix, Mongraal, Ares, rockit and Benjy at the Frankfurt bootcamp . Photo credit benjyfishy.

> " **Going to frankfurt to play on 0 ping in only 2 days let's gooooooo ooooooooooooooooo oooooooooo!** "
>
> *Benjy*

Anne: 'Having arrived in Frankfurt everything initially went well. However while they were there, Epic made some controversial changes to the Turbo Build delay settings. Epic subsequently reverted the changes, but by that time Benjy and Kyle had already made the decision to cut their month-long bootcamp short and return home to the UK, while Dimitri stayed in Frankfurt.

We had less than 24 hours to arrange the return flights from Germany. When Benjy arrived back in the UK a couple of days later, he announced that he was going to a bootcamp in London. However after the arrangements were made and he arrived in London, he changed his mind and decided that he preferred to play from home and so after 48 hours he came back.'

Martin also visited the Frankfurt bootcamp during the finals of the Trios FNCS.

Bootcamps or team houses are less common in Fortnite than for other esports games, such as CS:GO, Call of Duty and Overwatch, due to the fact they are specific four-or-five player teams. Fortnite players tend to primarily practise locally from their homes. When a bootcamp is organised it is a great opportunity for players to finally play together, perfect their strategies and generally bond with each other in real life.

Players may also change teammates depending on the different Fortnite seasons and quite often they will play for different organisations. For example, Benjy is with NRG, Mongraal is with FaZe and Mitr0 is with Team Liquid.

0 ping/Frankfurt, Martin. Photo credit MrSavage.

MONGRAAL–MITRO–BENJYFISHY–MRSAVAGE

Anne: 'The decision for Benjy to switch partners from Martin, to play trios with Mongraal and Mitr0 (MMB) and then duos with Kyle before the FNCS Season X in 2019, was something that Johnny and I were fully aware of. We were in communication about the situation and as parents, we both understood that we cannot and should not influence who our children play with, as it is a hundred per cent their decision. They are professional players who desire to remain at the top, so if they feel that a Fortnite season requires a different partnership, then they will discuss this between themselves.'

Johnny: 'Martin had played with Benjy and Mongraal in a trio cash cup during the lead-up to the World Cup, but he was not available for all of the events due to various mandatory school trips. Subsequently, Benjy and Mongraal decided to play with Mitr0 in Martin's absence.'

Anne: 'Once the FNCS Trios was announced, Benjy and Kyle felt that they played better

with Dmitri and so made the switch. Ultimately the MMB trio had great success that season and dominated the tournament during the heats. However, even though they went into the finals as one of the favourites, they experienced some bad luck and were overpowered by mechs (the controversial giant robots were removed from the game in the following season) and were denied the trophy.'

Johnny: 'In the end, Martin's trio with Dave "Rojo" Jong and Calum "Itemm" MacGillivray finished in 7th place and MMB finished in 10th place. They all remained friends. Anne and I also continued to stay in touch and it made no difference to our friendship and collaboration.'

> **"** *Obviously no beef between Mongraal, benjyfishy and I. Love both of you guys.* ❤️ *Hope the new trio works out in ur favour.* **"**
>
> *Martin*

> **"** *Legit nothing but love bro* ❤️
>
> *There is no beef between me and savage, we are still great friends we just feel like this is the better choice.* **"**
>
> *Mongraal*

> **"** *u guys gonna slay ly man.* **"**
>
> *Benjy*

At the hotel lobby in New York City 2019. From left to right: Mitr0, Mongraal, Martin and Benjy. Photo credit MrSavage.

In Chapter 2 Season 3 and 4, Martin and Benjy reunited and formed a new trio with Kevin "Letshe" Fedjuschkin for the FNCS Trios 2020.

BRING YOUR OWN COMPUTER (BYOC) LAN EVENTS
DREAMHACK WINTER, JÖNKÖPING, SWEDEN

Anne: 'The DreamHack tournament in Jönköping (28th November–1st December 2019) was the first time we had attended a Bring Your Own Computer (BYOC) LAN event. Being overseas brought another whole new dimension of challenges into the equation, in particular the question of how to hire the equipment. Both DreamHack events in Jönköping, Sweden and in Anaheim, USA involved getting equipment hired for the events.'

Johnny: 'As we live in Norway, it was easier for us to drive to the event in Sweden with Martin's computer. However, as Anne and Benjy flew in from the UK, they hired equipment from the event organisers.'

Anne: 'One of the things we didn't realise at DreamHack, was that you only get a basic chair to sit on during the event and for a professional player it is important to hire a proper gaming chair. We also didn't know that when you are given a chair, it is quite often not pre-built and you have to assemble it yourself. Not an ideal situation, especially if you arrive late and the hall is in darkness.'

Martin watching Benjy play at DreamHack Jönköping. Photo credit benjyfishy.

The key to hiring equipment at a BYOC event is preparation and making sure you book everything as early as possible due to limited availability. Not only do you have to think about sourcing the computer and monitor, but also chairs and the logistics of transporting the equipment from the collection point to your seat in the main hall.

Johnny: 'If you are planning on taking part in the tournaments at the LAN events, preparation is key. When you book your ticket, consider selecting a hall that doesn't have music playing from the main stage, as this can be a distraction. It is a good idea to take along in-ear headphones, along with a noise-cancelling over-ear set, to help with any excess noise. Space is limited at the events to just the players, so parents must base themselves outside of the main player areas.'

Anne: 'Once you have managed to co-ordinate and set up everything at the event, LANs are an invaluable opportunity for the players and parents to socialise and hang out together. Both Benjy and Martin had an amazing time in Sweden and really enjoyed the experience.'

TOP TIPS

1 Book early as spaces are limited.

2 If you need to hire equipment do this asap, as supplies are limited.

3 Check if you need to hire a gaming chair.

4 Book accommodation early, as hotels get booked out.

5 Research a suitable hall at the venue to sit in. Consider coordinating seating with your friends.

6 Bring with you LAN cables, travel adapter extension leads and hand warmers, as the halls can be cold.

7 Bring a flashlight, as the light generated by phones is not strong enough.

1st day of DreamHack Winter, Jönköping, Sweden, 2019. Photo credit benjyfishy (obviously).

Photo credit benjyfishy.

❝ **The last couple days have been some of the best days of my life. So many friends that I got to meet again, got to compete, placed decent while having a lot of fun. Love all of you guys for making this possible for me** ❤️❤️❤️. ❞

Martin

131

> **"** **Travelling the world to play a game that I love is the coolest thing, I love it. "**
>
> *Benjy*

MAXN...

TOP TIPS

1 Listen and abide by the rules.

2 Confirm what you are allowed to take on the main stage.

3 Carry peripherals in hand luggage, in case your suitcase gets lost and you can't get replacements.

4 Research possible gaming centres that you can practise in during lead-up to the event.

Photo credit Tennis Australia.

TRAVELLING

Players often look forward to the travelling element of international tournaments, as they can meet up with their friends from their geographic Fortnite region but also from other international regions as well.

BYOC events like DreamHack are much more relaxed than larger official LAN tournaments and players are able to interact with each other during the matches. However, this is not the case in the formal setting of larger tournaments where the players are on a stage.

AUSTRALIAN AO SUMMER SMASH

Anne: 'In early February 2020, Benjy was invited to the Australian Open (AO) Summer Smash, held at Melbourne Park. Even though Benjy usually really enjoys the travel aspect of LAN events, this time he was concerned about the long distance and the flight duration of over twenty hours. It took him a really long time to decide whether

he actually wanted to go. In the end, he reached out to his fans on Twitter and asked them whether they thought he should travel. The fans responded with a resounding yes.

Benjy was really pleased he had set aside his concerns and decided to travel, as the Summer Smash turned out to be one of his favourite events. On arrival, we met the event organisers at the airport and they took us to our hotel. The following day, we got to see the venue for the first time and Benjy took part in a press conference with a few other players.

The event was held over two days. The first day was the Charity Pro-Am Trio event, where Benjy teamed up with the former New Zealand professional racing car driver Richie Stanaway and Australian content creator Aliythia. Benjy managed to teach his teammates how to coordinate a grenade shot, to wipe out the opposing team. Despite an excellent performance, the team narrowly missed out on victory in the event, ending up in second place.

The second day was the solo event where Benjy finished 13th.'

From left to right: Nyhrox, Airwakes, Ceice, Replays, Jaomock, Benjy, Elevate. Photo credit Tennis Australia.

DREAMHACK ANAHEIM

Johnny: 'We arrived in Los Angeles a few days early before the DreamHack BYOC Anaheim event, which took place over three days, 21st–23rd February 2020. Martin was about to sign with 100 Thieves and he was able to spend some time at their Cash App Compound before the tournament and they were able to organise all kits for their players.

About 1200 players participated in the event, with 400 making it to the semi-finals and 100 to the finals of the competition. Since this was a LAN festival with players and spectators passing freely by the players' seats, we wanted to make sure that nobody incidentally bumped into Martin. Therefore, Martin's manager Peter sat close to him during all stages and I sat with him during the finals.

Martin finished in first place for the overall tournament which was a very special moment for him. In the final moments leading up to Martin's Victory Royale in the last game, there was a battle between Benjy and Martin, unfortunately resulting in Martin taking out Benjy. The 100 Thieves film crew did an amazing job capturing the whole drama – you will find it on their YouTube channel.'

Anne: 'Benjy came first in the semi-finals, but sadly experienced a loading bug during the finals so he missed a whole game. He managed to finish in 11th place, which was a huge achievement. Hopefully it is Benjy's time at the next tournament!'

Johnny: 'In retrospect, seeing Martin having fun and practising with his friends, in a positive and creative atmosphere for a whole week, was probably a key ingredient to his first place achievement. As a father it was heart-warming for me to see my son so happy—there is simply nothing more to ask for.'

TOP TIPS FOR PARENTS

1 In the days before a big tournament, offer extra support to your child by facilitating all practicalities.

2 Don't push your child or project any of your expectations on them, as they know what is at stake.

3 Try to act normal and be there for them. Give them space if they need it.

4 Book a decent hotel close to the event for convenience. Don't waste energy on unnecessary travel.

TOP TIPS FOR PLAYERS

1 Arrive early. If you have travelled across time zones you will need a few days to recover.

2 Don't practise 24/7. Take breaks and do relaxing activities that clear your head.

3 Meet friends, but don't overdo it. Don't forget to conserve your energy.

4 Surround yourself with positive people if you can.

5 Try to rest and get enough sleep. Eat and drink healthily and try to plan your meals.

The 100 Thieves team at DreamHack Anaheim 2020. From left to right (back): Brett "Grandmateets" Squires, Hayden "Elevate" Krueger, Martin, Johnny, Peter. From left to right (front): Andrew Vong, Anna Molly, Celina Wang, Brendan "Falconer" Falconer, Ryan Martineau. Photo credit 100 Thieves.

❝ You definitely feel worse for people when you eliminate them in a bigger event. When I see that it pops up with my friend's name, ahhh, why couldn't it have been someone else, right?!?

Because obviously I don't want them to do bad. 🇯🇯

Martin

TWITCHCON SAN DIEGO

Twitch is a live streaming platform owned by Amazon. In 2019, Twitch hosted a convention in both Europe and the USA, as a way of bringing the community together: to meet streamers, play games and watch esports, as well as socialise with friends. In September 2019, TwitchCon was held at the San Diego Convention Center.

Both Benjy and Martin managed to secure an invite to take part in the Twitch Rivals Fortnite Showdown, which was a trios event where 160 streamers came together to compete for a $400k prize pool.

Anne: 'Benjy was in the middle of filming "Stories from the Battle Bus" (a post-World Cup 2019 follow-up video) for Epic Games, so the film crew joined us out in San Diego to continue filming and were able to meet us at Twitch Rivals. Martin was also filming a video log (vlog) of the event.'

TWITCH RIVALS

Johnny: 'There were six matches in the Grand Finals, but games 2 and 3 stood out as especially memorable matches. In game 2, Martin's team came out with the Victory Royale.'

Anne: 'In game 3, Benjy was battling it out in a 1v1 with FaZe Danny "Dubs" Walsh, however he sadly just missed out on the victory. Both matches were very exciting and had our hearts racing.'

In the end, Martin's team placed 3rd while Benjy's placed 6th.

> " *I didn't perform as well as I wanted at World Cup but the fact that I played good at a LAN... I'm so happy, I'm so happy.* "
>
> *Benjy*

Martin with his 3rd place medal. Photo credit Aaron Mendez Films.

TWITCH RIVALS RESULTS

#1	Tina, Rhux, 1400pika	$117,000
#2	Dubs, Megga, ajo1x	$97,000
#3	MrSavage, KingRichard, rojo11	$88,000
#4	Agholor, xExoph, iMrSharpShooter	$88,000
#5	Blakeps, hking, ohreckz	$80,500
#6	MckyTV, Noward, benjyfishy	$69,000

Johnny's view from his seat at the Twitch Rivals stadium. Photo credit Aaron Mendez Films.

Top Creator Trios

Top Creator Trios

NRG FILMING

Johnny: 'While at TwitchCon, NRG had arranged to do some filming at Martin's Airbnb where he amusingly tried to teach the Fortnite team some words in Norwegian. This video is available on NRG's YouTube channel.'

Martin trying to teach Benjy some Norwegian! Photo credit MrSavage.

EQUIPMENT

If you are looking to become a professional player, content creator or involved in esports generally, having the right setup that works for you is an important ingredient.

Benjy and Martin's individual setups are considered top of the range, however they did not start out with this kit and there is a variety of equipment that will work for lower budgets.

Martin at his studio back home in February 2021, getting ready to practise some Fortnite. Photo credit MrSavage.

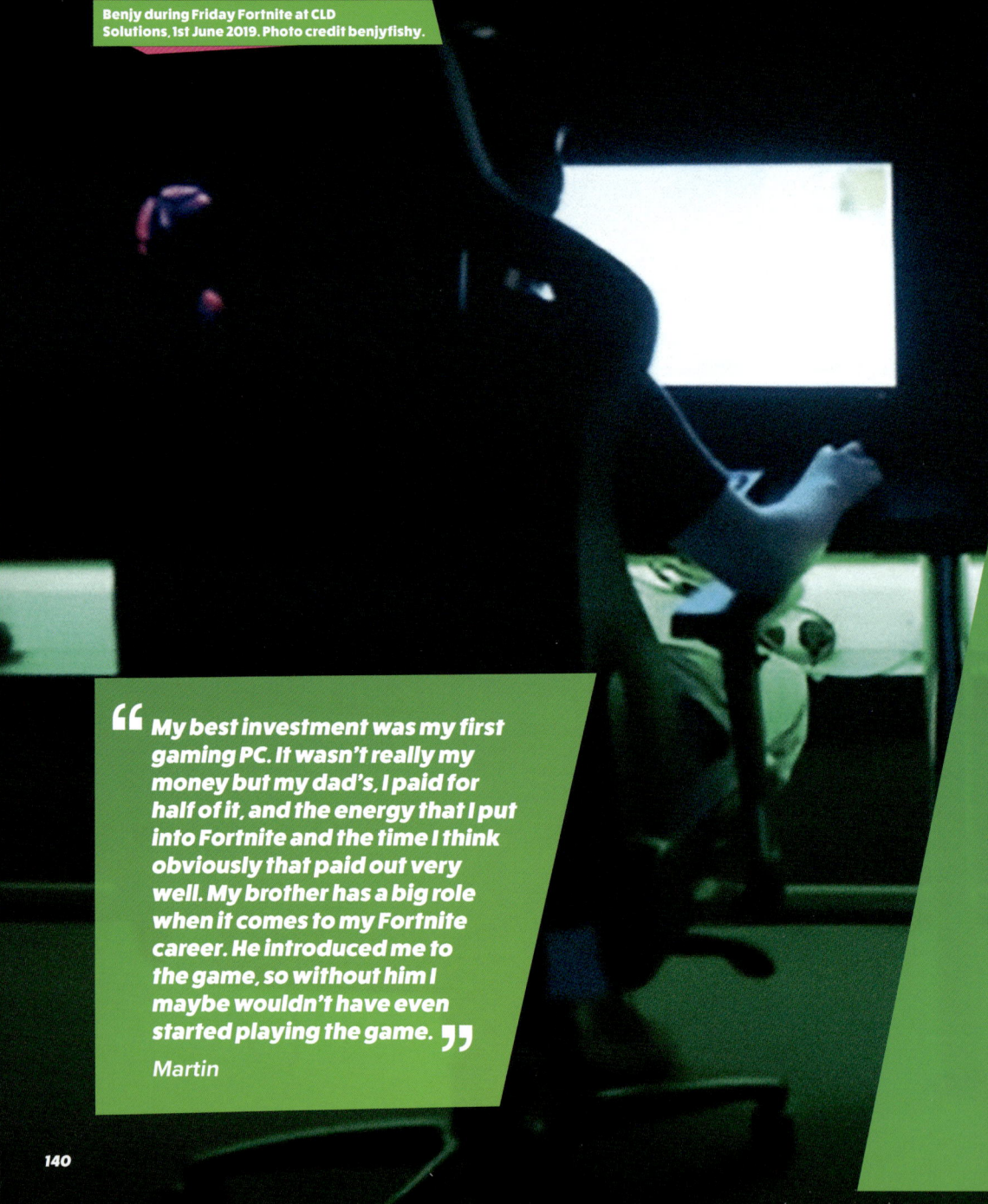

" *My best investment was my first gaming PC. It wasn't really my money but my dad's, I paid for half of it, and the energy that I put into Fortnite and the time I think obviously that paid out very well. My brother has a big role when it comes to my Fortnite career. He introduced me to the game, so without him I maybe wouldn't have even started playing the game.* "

Martin

BENJY AND MARTIN'S DEVICES

Both Benjy and Martin have played games for fun on numerous devices before their breakthrough.

Johnny: 'Martin used to bring his Nintendo DS everywhere he went so it he could play it on the go. While at home, he would play on his Nintendo Wii and various generations of PlayStation, until he was introduced to Minecraft which he played on a PC.'

Martin back in 2013–eight years old–playing Minecraft on an old computer. The monitor reads "You have won this match!". Photo credit Johnny Troset Andersen.

Anne: 'Benjy has a very similar background to Martin, but in addition he did have a try on the Xbox and Nintendo 64 consoles.'

Johnny: 'Martin's first gaming PC was a local Norwegian brand, Komplett, with an Intel i7-8700K CPU, 16 GB RAM and a 256 GB SSD on top of an ASUS TUF Z370-Plus motherboard and with an ASUS GeForce GTX 1080 TURBO graphic card.'

Anne: 'Benjy's first gaming PC was an Dell Alienware Aurora R5 with Intel i5-6400, 8GB RAM and with a NVIDIA GeForce GTX 970 graphic card.'

FORTNITE PLATFORMS

Fortnite is available on multiple platforms like Android devices, gaming consoles (Xbox, PlayStation and Nintendo Switch) and personal computers (Windows PCs and Macs). Both Benjy and Martin are Windows PC players.

Players can play against each other across these platforms, which makes it easy for friends to join in and adds to the popularity of the game. In 2020 there was an increase in the number of players taking part in tournaments across all the Fortnite regions. However, there are differences in the playability of the game on various platforms. Some competitions have separate leader boards per platform, whereas others combine all platforms together.

> **My brother introduced me to gaming. The first games I played were on the PS2, PS3, like Guitar Hero. I have been playing games since I was about five.**
>
> *Benjy*

The number of players on the Fortnite competitive scene is growing. From August 2019 to July 2021 almost seven times as many players took part in Week 1 Session 1 of Trio FNCS across all regions.

FNCS TRIO CHAPTER 1 - SEASON X - WEEK 1 - SESSION 1 (AUG 2019)
36,717 PLAYERS COMPETING

FNCS TRIO CHAPTER 2 - SEASON 7 - WEEK 1 - SESSION 1 (OCT 2020)
232,620 PLAYERS COMPETING

Data from fortnitetracker.com.

MONITOR REFRESH RATES

The casual observer may think that a monitor is just a monitor, right? Everyone has a flat LCD screen these days, so surely you can just grab any monitor and start playing? Well you can, but if you are aiming to become a professional player, having a monitor with a high refresh rate is a key ingredient to success.

The refresh rate is the number of times in a second that a display is illuminated and is measured in Hertz (Hz). Therefore a higher refresh rate allows for a player to see the movements of their opponents on screen more often, allowing for easier visual tracking of the player's target during fast-paced action, which again leads to a competitive advantage.

Gaming equipment retailers offer refresh rates in the range from 50–360 Hz, typically in the 144–165 Hz range. For esports 240 to 360 Hz are more suitable.

RESOLUTION

The higher the resolution, i.e. the screen width and height in picture elements (pixels), the more pages and words you can fit onto a screen, reducing the size of letters so they remain legible. Students, as well as office workers, tend to use high-resolution computers for multiple page documents. Higher resolutions are more demanding for the computer and not optimal for fast-paced games like Fortnite and is why players use low resolutions on their screens.

MARTIN'S MONITOR

Johnny: 'Martin's first monitor was 165 Hz (Acer 27" Predator) which I helped him to buy in January 2018 to complement his first gaming PC. I thought it would be good enough but past a certain age (my age, that is!) it seems that you are unable to see the difference between 165 Hz and higher refresh rates. Martin's current monitor is 360 Hz.

Martin's main monitor to the right. The monitor to the left is for non-gaming applications, like Discord (See Social Media chapter, page 186). Photo credit MrSavage.

Martin was once offered a curved monitor, but he refused since he was afraid it would distort his vision. In general, curved screens are wider which can put more strain on a gamer's field-of-view; they are also more prone to glare because they catch more angles. Not many professional players tend to use this option at tournaments and LANs, possibly because they are more expensive and therefore less available.'

MAKE SURE YOUR COMPUTER CAN HANDLE A HIGHER REFRESH RATE

Check with your retailer or tech savvy friend if your computer can handle the higher refresh rate. Your computer might need to be configured to utilize the higher refresh rate.

Both Benjy and Martin use a 1920 x 1080 (width x height) resolution, which is lower than many people use on their desktop PCs (2560 x 1440).

TOURNAMENTS

When you go to tournaments you do not always get a choice of monitor and so bringing your own could be a sensible option. However this is not always practical, for instance, during the Australian Open Summer Smash 2020 Tournament in Melbourne, Benjy and the other players had no other option but to use a 144 Hz monitor and a slower computer.

BENJY'S MONITOR

Anne: 'Benjy has mainly used standard monitors migrating from 60 Hz to 144 Hz and in 2019 he switched to 240 Hz. During that time he noticed a huge improvement when gaming.'

Benjy at his desk at home, July 2021. Photo credit Emily Mudie Photography.

" BTW to all of you guys who are on 60hz, you are at a MAJOR disadvantage, please, buy a 144hz monitor. If you don't have enough to buy one right now, its 100% worth it to save up any money to buy one if you want to get better. "

Benjy

Benjy's monitor is an HP Omen X25F. Photo credit NRG.

HEADSETS

The majority of young people will opt for headphones over speakers whether they are in school lessons, playing games, watching a movie, listening to music or just chatting to friends. The immersive experience allows them to sit for many hours at a time, therefore choosing the right headphones both for comfort and to protect your hearing is paramount and will help prevent long-term hearing loss.

In 2015, The World Health Organisation (WHO) estimated that more than a billion young people worldwide could be at risk of hearing loss due to unsafe listening practises. The daily limit for a safe volume level of any sound is below 85 decibels (dB) for a maximum duration of eight hours. The noise level of 85 dB roughly corresponds to heavy traffic, a noisy restaurant, or a gasoline powered lawn mower.

IMPORTANT FACTORS TO TAKE INTO CONSIDERATION WHEN CHOOSING A HEADSET:

 COMFORT

 SIZE

 DESIGN

 NOISE CANCELLATION

 WIRELESS OR WIRED

 GLASSES FRIENDLY

 **PRICE POINT**

It is advisable to go to a retailer to try out headsets before you buy. Get expert advice or even borrow a set from friends. However even though a headset fits your best friend it doesn't mean it will fit you – a bad fit can actually be physically painful after a few hours. Keep in mind that new and more comfortable pads can be bought separately.

Listening to in-game noises and being able to distinguish between them is crucial to a player's success. For example, footsteps will let you know if an opponent is close by, or identifying the type of weapon that is being used can ultimately help to claim the victory. If you are playing in team mode, being able to communicate effectively with other members is a key component.

At LAN competitions, wireless peripherals can suffer from interference with other similar devices and stop working.

Due to sound levels within the tournament venue, you may want to consider headsets with noise cancellation to be able to hear gameplay and teammates.. An alternative is to use in-ear headphones inside your normal headset (with your normal headset turned off), which is what Benjy has used during competitions. Benjy and Martin both travel with a pair of SHURE Sound Isolating Earphones for this purpose. However, we do not recommend using such in-ear headphones more than necessary, since they are at a greater risk of damaging your ears than over-the-ear headphones.

For parents of younger players who are concerned with online safety at home, there is the option to setup a console or computer with the sound playing from external speakers as well as the headset, so you can hear what other players are saying to your child.

TOP TIPS

Martin at DreamHack Anaheim 2020. Photo credit 100 Thieves.

Take a couple of minutes' break from your headset at least once every hour. **1**

Turn down the volume or set a volume limit. **2**

Use noise-cancelling headphones. **3**

Alternate between headphone use and speaker use. **4**

Ensure headphones are not too heavy and fit comfortably over your ears. **5**

Consider wireless headphones for young gamers as wires can be a trip hazard. **6**

Buying new pads can extend the life of your old headset and save you money. **7**

Martin uses the ROCCAT Khan AIMO.

Benjy uses the Turtle Beach Elite Atlas Aero Wireless.

Photo credit Emily Mudie Photography.

#HEADSETCHALLENGE

In April 2020 both Martin and Emil "Nyhrox" Bergquist completed a challenge to play Fortnite without the use of their headsets. It was organised by the Norwegian HLF (The Norwegian Association for the Hard of Hearing) to promote awareness of hearing damage among young people and the campaign reached more than 3.2 million gamers worldwide.

KEYBOARDS

The choice of peripherals, including keyboard, mouse and headset, comes down to individual preference as every player has their unique way of positioning them on their desk.

Anne: 'At the World Cup in 2019, Johnny and I were both surprised by the different peripherals setups. For example, we both naturally assumed that everyone used their keyboards in the traditional horizontal position, only to find that this is not the case. Just taking into account the NRG roster there is a big difference in the way the players use their keyboards.'

Johnny: 'Benjy and Martin both use their keyboards in the more traditional horizontal style, but Martin has started to angle his a little bit lately.'

Positioning your keyboard at an angle creates more space between your mouse and the keyboard. It also gives your thumb better access to more keys, which may be useful in Fortnite, due to the number of keys required to play. However, it may put more strain on your wrist, so try it out carefully by increasing the angle gradually.

Putting the keyboard at a horizontal angle, as both Benjy and Martin do, also has its advantages. It is maybe the most natural position, and it also doesn't take up much space vertically on your desk.

Selecting the right keyboard is about tactile feel and feedback, but also speed. Both Benjy and Martin prefer mechanical keyboards as they are faster than membrane keyboards. Mechanical keyboards are characterised by a distinctive click feeling as each key comes

Shane "EpikWhale" Cotton uses his keyboard vertically. Photo credit NRG.

Williams "Zayt" Aubin uses his keyboard at an angle and sits very close to the monitor. Photo credit NRG.

Martin uses the keyboard in the more traditional horizontal style . Photo credit MrSavage.

Benjy's positioning of his keyboard – quite similar to Martin's. Photo credit benjyfishy.

with a switch. These tend to be noisier than their membrane counterparts, which protect against spills and are lighter. Again, it boils down to comfort, what feels right and what you are used to.'

KEYBINDS

Johnny: 'Keybinds are the mapping of keys on the keyboard and mouse to in-game controls. There is an on-going debate online regarding the best keybinds configuration, considering aspects such as length of fingers, size of keyboard and which angles to use.

You can find both Benjy and Martin's individual keybinds online by searching "benjyfishy settings" and "MrSavage settings".'

There are different sized keyboards, which are popular among gamers, ranging from 40% – 75% of a full-sized keyboard.

Benjy and Martin use a keyboard without a number pad, which is known as a "tenkeyless" (TKL) keyboard.

Benjy uses the Apex Pro TKL while Martin uses the ROCCAT Vulcan TKL Pro.

BENJY	CONTROL	MARTIN
Q	Wall	F
Mouse button 5	Floor	G
C	Stairs	T
Left Shift	Roof	Left Shift
V	Trap	F5
Mouse wheel down	Use	E
Left ctrl	Crouch	Left ctrl
Tab	Inventory	Tab
M	Map	F1
R	Reload/Rotate	Y
E	Building Edit	R
Off	Confirm Edit on Release	Off
1	Harvesting Tool	1
2	Weapon Slot 1	2
3	Weapon Slot 2	3
4	Weapon Slot 3	4
5	Weapon Slot 4	5
Z	Weapon Slot 5	6

GAMING MOUSE

There is a wide range of gaming PC mice available on the market, so a player should consider the following factors before making a purchase:

 WIRED OR WIRELESS

 SENSITIVITY

 GRIP STYLE

 SHAPE, SIZE AND WEIGHT

Sensors on a gaming mouse are designed to be more responsive and accurate than a traditional mouse and tend to have more buttons on them.

WIRED OR WIRELESS

Anne: 'Benjy has used both wired and wireless mice, however due to the interference at LAN tournaments he now uses a wired mouse.'

Johnny: 'Martin has always opted for a wired mouse to avoid the hassle of recharging or changing batteries.'

A wireless mouse can be more versatile with higher latency whereas a wired mouse has faster response times but the cable can get in the way. Both Benjy and Martin use a mouse bungee for the cable to alleviate this.

SENSITIVITY

Mouse sensitivity relates to how the movement of your mouse on your desk, corresponds to movement on screen. Finding a mouse sensitivity ('sens') that suits you is important when gaming. High sensitivity gives you more control over directional adjustments, while low sensitivity gives you more control of your aim. These are conflicting requirements and as a result there is a lot of online debate and analysis of professional players' mouse settings.

Low sensitivity players tend to use large sweeping motions across large distances by using their entire arm to move the mouse. Low sensitivity allows you to shoot with more precision.

High sensitivity players usually use their hand and wrist to make most of their mouse movements instead of their whole arm. In Fortnite, high sensitivity is good for quick turns and builds.

Both Benjy and Martin use high sensitivity.

BENJY	FORTNITE MOUSE SETTING	MARTIN
800	DPI	1450
500	Hz	1000
14%	X-Axis Sensitivity	8.1%
14%	Y-Axis Sensitivity	8.1%
70%	Targeting Sensitivity	70%
70%	Scope Sensitivity	95%

Sensitivity is not a single number, but made up of X-Axis, Y-Axis, Targeting, Scope sensitivity and DPI.

LEFT-HANDED GAMING MOUSE

A selection of manufacturers such as Razer, Logitech, Corsair, SteelSeries and ROCCAT have designed left-handed and ambidextrous mice for gaming.

GRIP STYLE

How you hold your mouse can make a difference in your reaction time, agility and comfort. There are three main styles of mouse grip:

CLAW \ PALM \ FINGERTIP

For palm or claw grip a heavier, larger mouse is worth considering. If you use a fingertip grip then a lightweight, smaller mouse may be more comfortable.

Martin has something in between a fingertip and claw grip style.

Benjy has a claw grip style.

SHAPE, SIZE AND WEIGHT

Pick a mouse that feels comfortable as well as having the buttons and functionality you need. Some mice have removable plates so you can adjust the mouse to your preferred weight.

Getting the right ergonomic mouse that works for you can help having issues in the future with repetitive strain injury (RSI).

TOP TIPS

1. Educate yourself about the different mouse sensitivity settings and how they work together.
2. Test different settings (including DPI) and establish what works best for you.
3. Don't be afraid to try out different brands. What feels right for you is most important.
4. Consider using mouse skates (which are attached to the base) to make your mouse slide better.

Benjy has an ENDGAME GEAR XM1 WHITE mouse.

Martin has a ROCCAT Kone Pure Ultra – White mouse.

Both mice are quite light. Benjy's weights 82 grams while Martin's weights 66 grams.

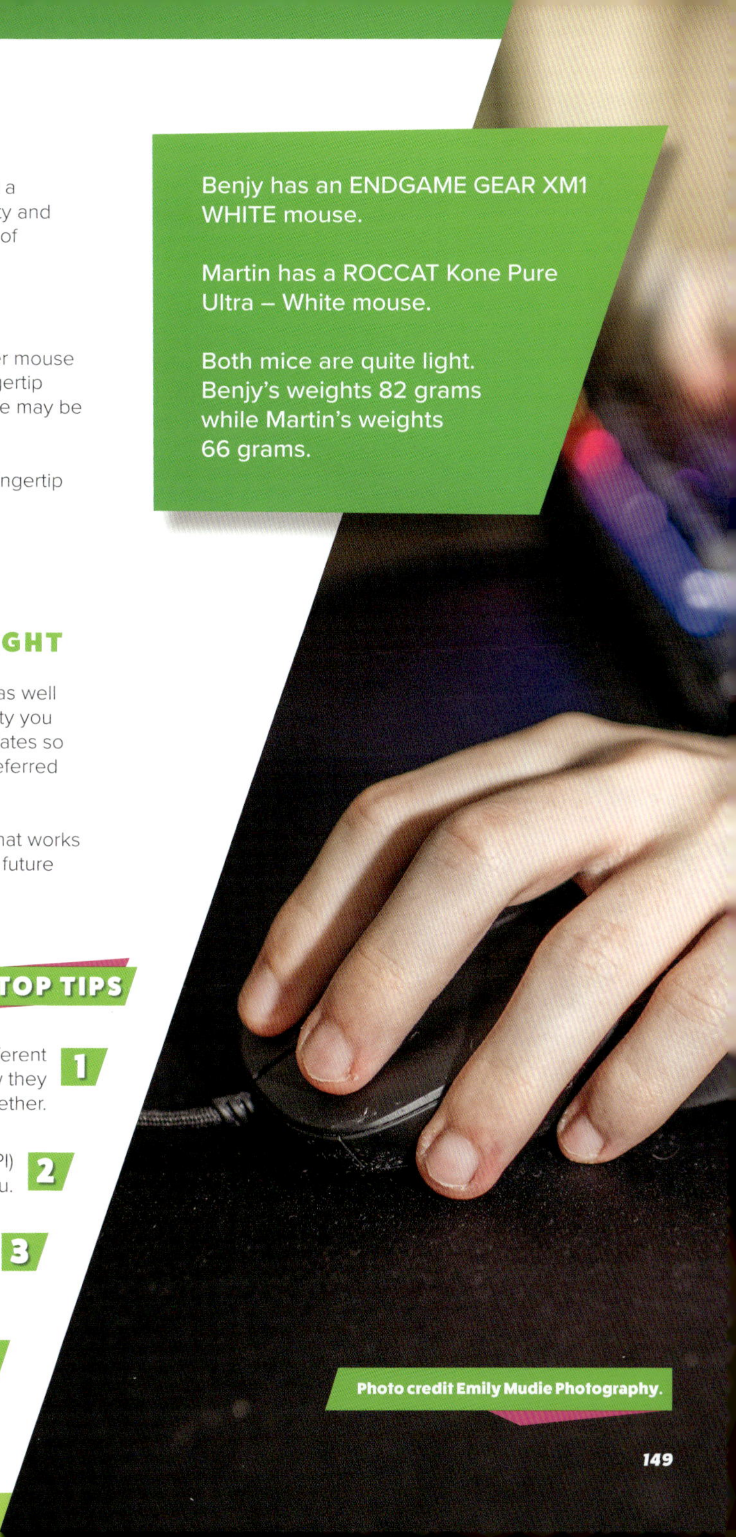

Photo credit Emily Mudie Photography.

STREAMING

Streaming allows you to showcase your gameplay through a live video. It allows you to demonstrate your gaming skills as well as your unique personality, in order to reach online viewers. Additionally, it enables you to chat and interact with your fans.

FIRST STEPS

In order to start streaming, you need to install software, like Streamlabs OBS, StreamElements or XSplit Gamecaster, on your PC. You also need to open an account on a live streaming service like Twitch or YouTube Live.

The streaming software must be set up in such a way that it does not drain Fortnite of the computing and graphics resources needed for displaying gameplay on your PC. At the same time the streaming software must provide the viewers with a decent video quality. It is a balancing act. The software Streamlabs OBS (which both Benjy and Martin use) has an Auto Optimize feature that can come in handy, as it automatically suggests the best settings for the player to use.

In the early days, Benjy and Martin started out without any cameras. This was because they wanted to gain confidence before taking the next step, which for many is to introduce a camera for their keyboard and mouse. Sometimes the boys still run streams with only a keyboard or mouse camera or none at all.

> **6 months ago I started streaming, I was averaging around 2 viewers per stream. I stopped for around 2-3 months, and had my first stream back today and averaged around 20 viewers which is insane for me, thank you for everyone who tuned in it means a lot.**
>
> *Benjy, November 2018*

FACECAM

Benjy and Martin had both been streaming for more than a year before they decided to take the next step to using a facecam, which was a huge milestone for both of them.

> **First facecam stream was really fun, going to be streaming sooooo much more, thank you to everyone who came and checked out the stream.**
>
> *Benjy*

Benjys first facecam stream. Photo credit benjyfishy.

> **Me and Mongraal started playing together alot on stream. This led me to averaging about 100 viewers.**
>
> *Martin*

STREAMING DURING COMPETITIONS

Streaming can easily put a mental burden on a player's gameplay especially in a competition. Your stream can be distracting, as you know that you have viewers so you need to check the online chat in between games and thank your fans for subscribing and supporting you. However, you also should be focusing on the tournament, reviewing your last game and improving your tactics for your next game.

You of course also reveal your gameplay patterns to competitors, who may watch your stream or uploaded videos afterwards, giving them an advantage over time.

Another consideration when streaming in competition is that you run the risk that some competitors might notice your position on the map (with just a few seconds' delay) thereby making you easier to eliminate. This banned practice known as 'stream sniping' can be alleviated by putting a longer delay on your stream of around 1 to 5 minutes before it reaches your viewers.

DIGITAL MILLENNIUM COPYRIGHT ACT (DMCA)

Be aware that copyright laws apply while streaming. Benjy and Martin are not allowed to play music on stream and they must take care that no one in their Discord group does either. The laws also mean that they cannot show copyrighted video content.

Additionally, this includes the licensed audio that appears in Fortnite, which the boys can switch off in their Fortnite settings.

> **" Wish I'd play as good on stream as I do off stream :/ sucks not being able to perform in cash cups and stuff while streaming. "**
>
> *Martin*

> **" Will be playing the duo event off stream, feels kinda s**t streaming when I know that I can play alot better off-stream, as soon as I turned off my stream yesterday, I played twice as good, hope you understand. "**
>
> *Benjy*

TOP TIPS GAINING VIEWERS

1 Keep to a regular streaming schedule.

2 Do not give up, even if you have few viewers.

3 Play games together with other streamers.

4 Stream for fun (your viewers will notice it if you do not have positive energy to share).

5 Use a facecam, if you are comfortable with it.

Martin at his studio desk at home, February 2020. Mounting, wiring, configuring and testing all his equipment from scratch would take a couple of days for a professional technician. Photo credit MrSavage.

DUAL PC SETUP

Professional streamers often invest in a separate PC for their streaming software, to offload their game PC and to prevent their Fortnite performance being affected at all. This also allows for improving the stream quality using higher bitrates and better video encoders and allowing them to record the stream to a local disk with an even higher bitrate.

The basic idea of a dual PC setup is to duplicate the gaming monitor video output through a second video port on your game PC. Such duplication comes built-in, with a graphic card and puts very little strain on the game PC. However a video capture card is required on the secondary, stream PC, to receive the duplicated video signal.

Martin's setup is illustrated in detail on the next page and commented below. Benjy has a dual setup available but prefers his single PC setup. So, a dual PC setup is by no means required.

MARTIN'S SETUP

- The audio from the microphone, the gameplay (Fortnite audio) and any teammates audio (Discord) on the game PC are synced to the same video output as the gameplay screen.

- The gameplay and teammate audio are forwarded to his headset. The audio wiring requires either a hardware audio mixer like the GoXLR or a software mixer like Voicemeeter, which Martin uses.

- Audio mixing can get complex and Martin has a checklist to help him out. He understands the setup on his game PC sufficiently to solve any audio mixer crashes or configuration adjustments between games.

- Martin's audio is divided into four separate tracks. An all-mixed audio track is fed, along with the video output cable, to the stream PC and immediately sent to the Twitch stream. The three other tracks (mic, Discord and Fortnite) feed over his local area network into a high-quality recording to local disk on the stream PC.

- After a stream Martin's recording is uploaded to his editors, who then are able to remove any accidental bad language from his teammates or himself, or crosstalk, by selectively muting the various audio tracks. This results in videos of higher overall quality. Videos without bad language also have a higher chance to reach a wider audience on YouTube.

- Martin has two cameras. One displays his face and upper body (facecam) and the second displays both his keyboard and mouse. Since he likes to stream with little or no lighting on, high quality cameras are required. These connect to the PCs over SDI, which has higher quality than USB and the additional advantage of supporting longer cables and extensions.

When designing Martin's setup, it was key to make sure his gameplay wasn't reliant on the stream PC in case of malfunction. When Martin is playing he depends on his headset, his microphone and his conversation with teammates through Discord, therefore these are connected to the game PC. Secondary or 'unnecessary' devices like cameras are connected to the stream PC.

Microphone
SHURE SM7B
w/ZOOM audio
converter

USB

Headset
ROCCAT Khan
Aimo

USB

**Gaming PC
monitor**

DisplayPort

Keyboard
ROCCAT TKL Pro

**Peripheral
switcher**

USB

Mouse
ROCCAT Ultra Pro

**SDI
Capture card**

VBAN   Menu   _   X

1   **3**   **5**   **7**

Mic
Line
(ZOOM UAC-2 Audio)

Discord
CABLE output
(VB-Audio Virt)

Not in use
Select input device

Game
Voicemeeter VIAO
44100Hz-7168

Voicemeeter VIAO
44100Hz-7168

A1 A2 A3   HARDWARE OUT 48kHz | 512
Elgato (NVIDIA High Def Audio)
Speakers (2-ROCCAT Khan AIMO)

INTELLIPAN   INTELLIPAN   INTELLIPAN   EQUALIZER   EQUALIZER

VOICE   Colour Panel
fx echo brightness
Lo   Hi

VOICE   Colour Panel
fx echo brightness
Lo   Hi

VOICE   Colour Panel
fx echo brightness
Lo   Hi

Treble 0.0
0.0
Bass 0.0

Treble 0.0
0.0
Bass 0.0

Click to Select Audio file for Playback
Or click on Record Button below
00:00
44100Hz   2Ch

A1
A2
A3
B1
B2

Displayport   **Video + all
audio mixed**

AUDIBILITY   AUDIBILITY   AUDIBILITY

Comp Gate   Comp Gate   Comp Gate

Front L R Rear   Front L R Rear   **6**

MASTER SECTION

Normal mode   MIX down A   Normal mode   Normal mode   Normal mode
mono   mono   mono   mono   mono
EQ   EQ   EQ   EQ   EQ
mute   mute   mute   mute   mute

9.0

0   0   0   0   0   0

A1   A1   A1   A1   A1
A2   A2   A2   A2   A2
A3   A3   A3   A3   A3
B1   B1   B1   B1   B1
B2   B2   B2   B2   B2
mono   mono   mono   M.C   K
solo   solo   solo   solo   solo
mute   mute   mute   mute   mute

Mic   Discord   Not in use   Game   Fader Gain

2   **4**

-50 A1   A2   -50 A1   -50 A1   -50 A1
0   0   0   0   0
Fader Gain   Fader Gain   Fader Gain   Fader Gain   Fader Gain

PHYSICAL   VIRTUAL

GAME PC

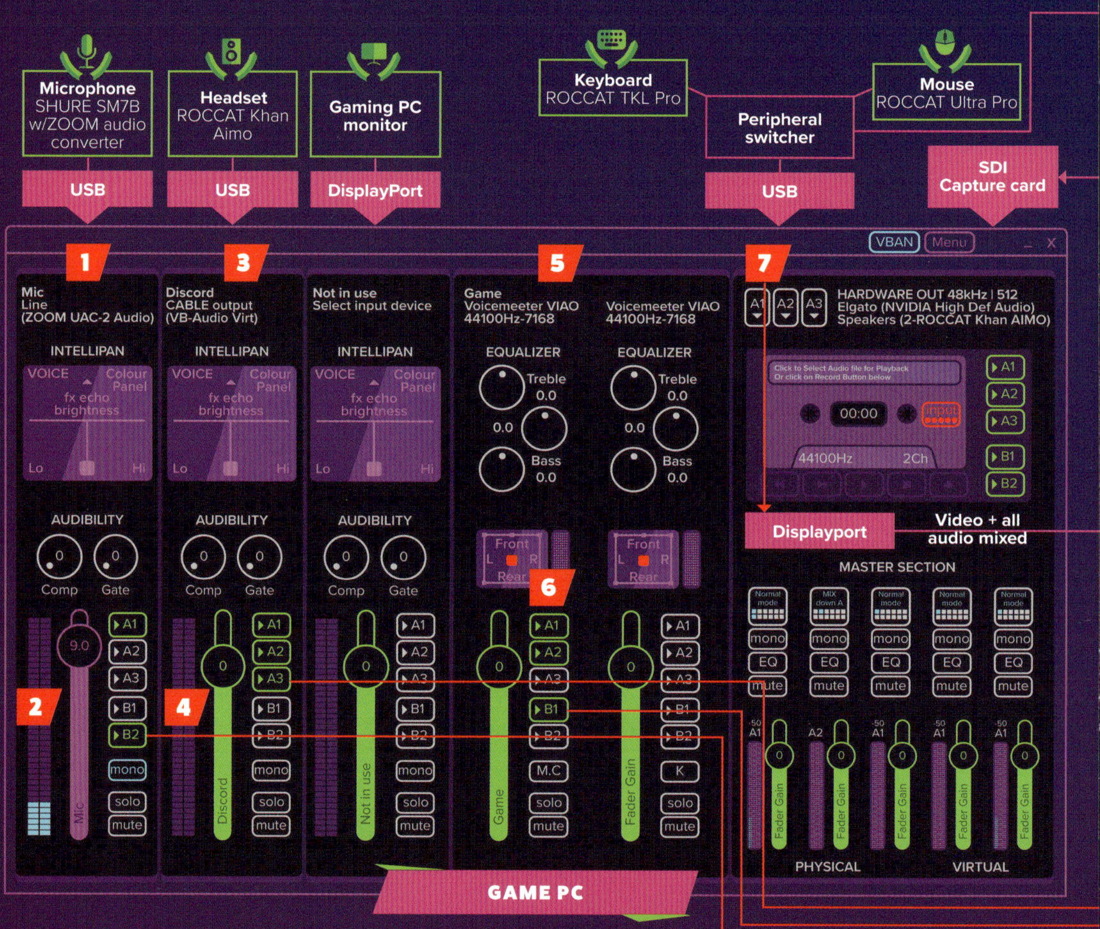

Hardware input 1:
The mic.   **1**

The mic is converted to mono and
amplified. Goes into bus A1 and B2.   **2**

Hardware input 2:   **3**
Teammates' audio from Discord.

Teammates' audio is sent
to bus A1, A2 and A3.   **4**

Virtual input 1: Audio from Fortnite
(and anything else from "within" the PC).   **5**

Fortnite audio goes into
bus A1, A2 and B1.   **6**

Hardware out A1 goes to the capture   **7**
card and is the mix of mic, teammates
audio and Fortnite audio. Hardware A2
goes to the headset and is the mix of
teammates audio and Fortnite audio.

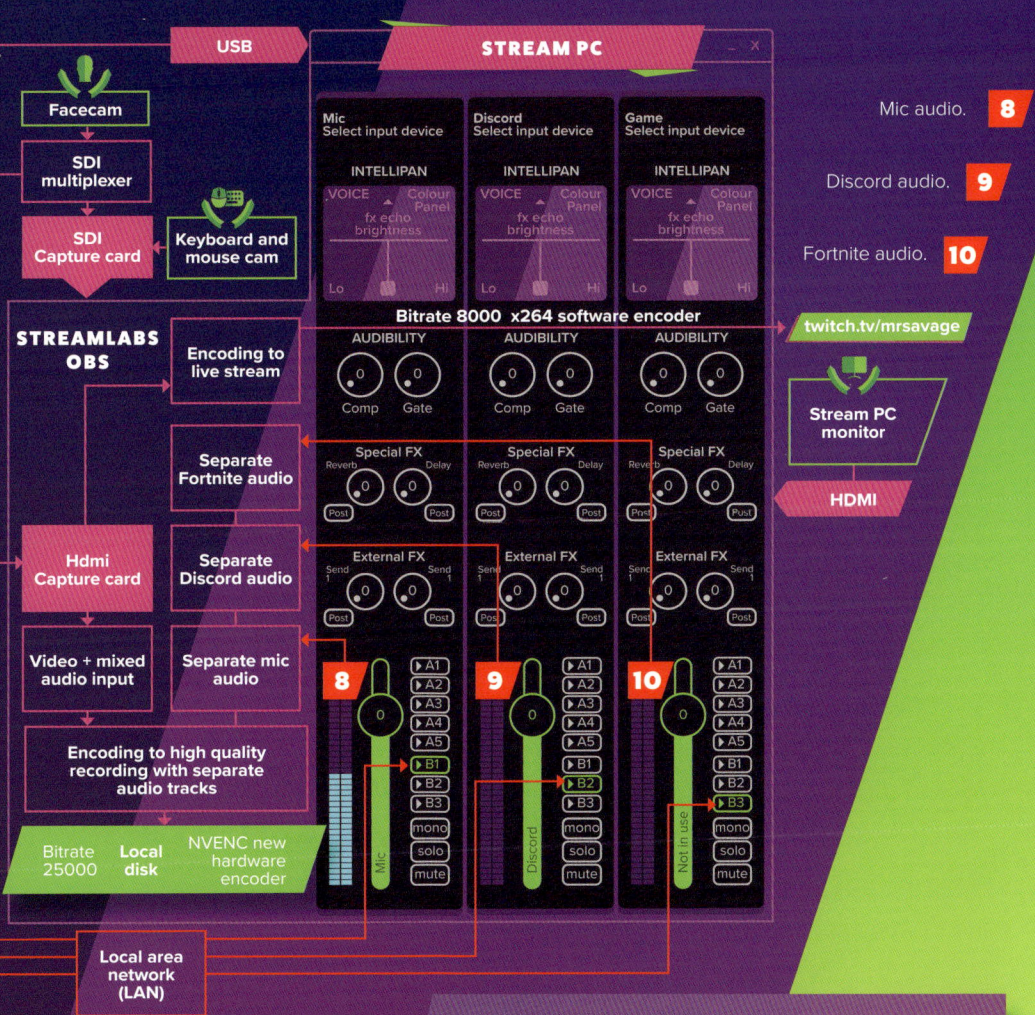

USB

STREAM PC

Facecam

SDI multiplexer

SDI Capture card

Keyboard and mouse cam

STREAMLABS OBS

Encoding to live stream

Separate Fortnite audio

Hdmi Capture card

Separate Discord audio

Video + mixed audio input

Separate mic audio

Encoding to high quality recording with separate audio tracks

Bitrate 25000 | **Local disk** | NVENC new hardware encoder

Local area network (LAN)

Mic
Select input device

Discord
Select input device

Game
Select input device

INTELLIPAN

VOICE — Colour Panel
fx echo brightness
Lo ▲ Hi

INTELLIPAN

VOICE — Colour Panel
fx echo brightness
Lo ▲ Hi

INTELLIPAN

VOICE — Colour Panel
fx echo brightness
Lo ▲ Hi

Bitrate 8000   x264 software encoder

AUDIBILITY
0 Comp 0 Gate

AUDIBILITY
0 Comp 0 Gate

AUDIBILITY
0 Comp 0 Gate

Special FX
Reverb 0 0 Delay
Post   Post

Special FX
Reverb 0 0 Delay
Post   Post

Special FX
Reverb 0 0 Delay
Post   Post

External FX
Send 1 0 0 Send 1
Post   Post

External FX
Send 1 0 0 Send 1
Post   Post

External FX
Send 1 0 0 Send 1
Post   Post

8 0
▶A1 ▶A2 ▶A3 ▶A4 ▶A5 ▶B1 ▶B2 ▶B3 mono solo mute
Mic

9 0
▶A1 ▶A2 ▶A3 ▶A4 ▶A5 ▶B1 ▶B2 ▶B3 mono solo mute
Discord

10 0
▶A1 ▶A2 ▶A3 ▶A4 ▶A5 ▶B1 ▶B2 ▶B3 mono solo mute
Not in use

Mic audio. **8**

Discord audio. **9**

Fortnite audio. **10**

twitch.tv/mrsavage

Stream PC monitor

HDMI

> **" We like to call those who stream in darkness, dungeon streamers. ""**
>
> *Richard Neumann at SUB2r, a San Francisco stream cam startup, commenting on Martin's tendency to turn off all lights in his room during competitive streams.*

155

CONTROLLERS

Not all PC players use a mouse and a keyboard as some controller devices have found their way to PCs. Controller devices were traditionally used on consoles like PlayStation and Xbox. Fortnite has in-game settings specifically for these devices and they plug into PCs just as mice and keyboards would do. Epic Games are trying to level the playing field so there is no advantage whether a player chooses to use a keyboard and mouse, or a controller device.

LIMITED FEATURES

Standard controllers have a limited number of buttons and features. Since Fortnite and many other games have a high number of functions that a player needs to simultaneously control, this has opened a market for third party vendors to deliver devices with extra buttons, adjustable triggers, configurable thumbsticks and paddles.

The base of a controller showing paddles providing more input features. Photo credit Anne Fish.

HYBRID PLAYERS

Before Epic Games adapted to facilitate the balance between controllers, and keyboard and mouse, some gamers became hybrid players, switching between the two types of input devices depending on the Fortnite season, some even switching mid-game. The best example of the latter is Shane "EpikWhale" Cotton, who was one of the first players to pick up a controller in close-range fights while using keyboard and mouse for building, editing and more.

NRG Esports made a video with EpikWhale explaining his thoughts behind his hybrid play.

AIM ASSIST CONTROVERSY

According to prosettings.net, about 3% of professional PC Fortnite players use a controller. This is not a significant number but has been enough to create a controversy within the professional Fortnite community. Due to the fact that aiming with a controller is harder than with a mouse, the "aim assist" setting was created inside Fortnite to automatically adjust the player's aim to improve their accuracy.

For a long time, the aim assist gave controller players a slight advantage, however when placing players in leaderboards Epic Games did not take this into account. Since then, Epic Games has slowly issued updates to fix the issue and create a more balanced gameplay between the two types of input devices.

CONSOLE VS PC

Whilst some players choose to use controller devices on a PC, there are a large number of players competing on a console with controllers. The global data from the FNCS Duos Warmup in March 2020 showed that there were more console duos competing than PC duos.

Regional Population - Duo FNCS Warmup March 2020:

	CONSOLE DUOS	PC DUOS	TOTAL DUOS	TOTAL PLAYERS	GLOBAL %
EU	46,904	54,966	101,870	203,740	54%
NAE	17,351	15,765	33,116	66,232	17%
BR	15,037	8,689	23,726	47,452	12%
AS	7,761	4,110	11,871	23,742	6%
NAW	5,677	5,555	11,232	22,464	6%
ME	2,307	2,471	4,778	9,556	3%
OC	1,762	1,651	3,413	6,826	2%
GLOBAL	96,799	93,207	190,006	380,012	

Data from fortnitetracker.com. Reproduced with permission from @FortniteBRLive

PROFESSIONAL CONTROLLER PLAYERS

The best-known professional players using controller on PC are Dominic "Unknown" Green, Jaden "Wolfiez" Ashman, and Nick "Nickmercs" Kolcheff.

Players may look to incorporate a controller player into their team, to assist with eliminations and any controller advantages. During the October 2020 Trios FNCS competition, Benjy and Martin teamed up with Kevin "Letshe" Fedjuschkin who is a controller player.

> **It made more sense to find a solo that can follow me and Savage and just copy our playstyle. That's pretty much how we got Letshe, he was the first person we tried out and it has just stuck ever since.**
>
> *Benjy*

> **Just got double dinked by EpikWhale and I was like "I guess he just has good aim" but then I go on his stream and he is playing controller. I'm so done with this loooooolk.**
>
> *Martin*

Photo credit Matilda Wormwood from Pexels.

INTERNET BROADBAND

A gamer's PC needs to be connected to a wired network, running all the way from their PC to the internet modem. Wifi is practical for general home and office use, but for professional gaming a wired connection is required, simply because it is faster and more reliable.

BANDWIDTH

Wired broadband connections come in a variety of packages and there is a lot to consider. For professional gaming, unlimited data plans are recommended, which will avoid suddenly being halted mid-game. The minimum bandwidth requirement for first shooter games like Fortnite seems to be a download speed of 3 Mbps and upload speed of 1 Mbps. Streaming your gameplay would add 5–15 Mbps.

Realistically you need even higher speeds than that, maybe a minimum of 30 Mbps for both download and upload. You also need to take into consideration having to download large game updates, while the rest of the household are working online or watching Netflix. Make sure it is possible to upgrade your speed if you run into bottlenecks. Average internet speeds are on the rise, but so are the bandwidth requirements as games are getting larger and platforms such as Netflix offering higher quality streams.

BACKUP LINE

For professional players internet outages during important online events, such as cups or sponsorship streams, can be costly. Therefore it is a good idea to have a backup connection line. Benjy has kept his old 5 Mbps wired connection, but also the mobile setup if his main line falls out. Martin has a 5G mobile connection configured in addition to his existing fibre connection.

PING

Ping means how fast data travels from your device to the internet server and back again so in terms of Fortnite, it is how fast the response is to an in-game action. This varies with the distance to the Fortnite servers, which in Europe are close to Paris, France. Benjy experiences a ping of 10-20 milliseconds, while Martin has 15-25 milliseconds. You can't do much about the distance to the servers, but you can make sure to select an Internet Service Provider with as low ping as possible.

> " If I could have a superpower it would be teleportation so I could teleport to every region and play every cash cup on 0 ping. "
>
> *Benjy*

Computer networking is a separate field of expertise. Consider consulting a local network expert if you need help. Photo credit Brett Sayles from Pexels.

BENJY AND MARTIN'S CONNECTIONS

Anne: 'Living on an island at the start of Benjy's career made getting internet both challenging and expensive. A newly dedicated leased line was installed which took approximately six months to organise. Before the new line Benjy had a 5 Mbps connection, which made streaming impossible except through an additional but weak mobile setup. After the line was installed Benjy's internet speed increased to around 100 Mbps.'

Johnny: 'My family live quite centrally in Oslo, Norway, and enjoys a high-quality fibre line from a local vendor. Martin's internet speed is 500 Mbps which is more than enough for gameplay and streaming and for the rest of the family.'

Both Benjy and Martin upload quite large gameplay recordings to their editors and download drafts for review.

EVERY MILLISECOND COUNTS

Johnny: 'The standard router devices installed in your home by Internet Service Providers are probably not optimized for gaming. A network expert replaced Martin's router device with one that was suited for professional or office use and this reduced the ping by 4 milliseconds on average.'

Several professional players, including Benjy and Martin, went to Frankfurt to play in the 2019 FNCS Trio Tournament, as it was closer to the Fortnite servers resulting in lower ping (see page 127).

Martin's router device (Ubiquiti EdgeRouter 12). Photo credit MrSavage.

KEEPING HEALTHY

For the casual observer it may appear that players just sit in front of their screens barely moving during competitions. In reality, the player is actually focusing intensely and coordinating up to 400 movements per minute, with amazingly fast hand-eye movements and reaction times. The skills demonstrated by some of the top esports players are like watching superstars in traditional sports as they perform miraculous feats to eliminate their opposition.

However after two to three hours of competitive play, a player's stress level can increase significantly and they are prone to fatigue. Therefore a player needs to keep both physically and mentally agile in order to sustain their high performance to claim the win.

The content in this chapter is for informational purposes only and should not be used to substitute medical professional advice.

Some information is referenced from Esports Healthcare. Visit www.esportshealthcare.com for further details on selected subjects featured in this chapter.

Martin playing table tennis with Benjy in May 2019 close to Benjy's home in Surrey, UK. Photo credit benjyfishy.

EXERCISE

Esports and gaming in general involves sitting at a computer or console for many hours. Regular exercise is important to maintain both physical and mental health. According to the UK National Health Service (NHS) teenagers should strive for at least 60 minutes of moderate to vigorous physical activity every day.

Exercise helps to maintain a healthy weight and lowers the risk of most diseases including type 2 diabetes and high blood pressure.

TAKING BREAKS

The most effective way to avoid injuries and fatigue is to take breaks and perform movements you normally do not do while gaming, for example look around the room, stand up and move, turn your head, or blink your eyes.

STRESS LEVELS

The University of Mississippi published a study in 2020, which revealed Fortnite players have a maximum heart rate of about 130 beats per minute during a competition.

With tournaments lasting anything from three to seven hours, maintaining focus and concentration as well as being able to manage the highs and lows of competition is incredibly hard. Exercise is therefore one of the best ways to help manage the impact of stress and improve focus.

ATHLETIC TRAINING

Many top-level esports teams and players include physical training and healthy eating in their regimes. Team houses incorporate gym areas for their players to use. When Benjy visited the FaZe House in Los Angeles during DreamHack Anaheim 2020 there was a complete work out area for the players to use.

Johnny: 'Martin does physical exercise at home. The exercises include rowing, walking and general strength training. He avoids exercises with grips similar to his keyboard or mouse grip, like tennis or racket ball (squash).'

Anne: 'Benjy trains every day, three times a week with a personal trainer and the rest of the week at home either cycling, walking or weight training.'

WARM-UP ROUTINE

All traditional sports acknowledge the need for preparing your body before a competition and esports is no exception. Players' routines involve warming up fingers, hands, wrists, forearms, and eyes. A good warm-up will make you feel loose and ready to play and avoid injuries.

Do a dynamic movement routine instead of a static stretching routine.

Mirror the movements of the game, either by doing exercises away from or with a keyboard and mouse.

Include focus and strengthening exercises for your eye muscles, to keep you vigilant.

Martin's warm-up routine can be found on his YouTube channel, 'How MrSavage Warms Up'.

COOL DOWN ROUTINE

A cool down routine is important after physical exercise and esports is no different. This will initiate your body's healing and recovery process and help prevent future injuries..

Esports Healthcare offer stretching exercises on their website and YouTube channel, 'Gamer Stretches (Cooldown)'.

Exercise can help maintain a fast reaction time while competing. When your body becomes fatigued, your brain functions slow down and therefore your reaction time goes down.

Martin working out at a local gym, Magnat Center in 2019. Photo credit Frang Foto.

EAT WELL, PLAY WELL

The stereotype of the lazy, inactive gamer living on fast food in their parents' house has quickly faded during the last few years. Professional players are well aware that a healthy diet is important for them especially when playing for long periods of time and often late into the evenings.

Some esports organisations hire professional chefs for their team houses to feed their players properly, as they acknowledge the role that balanced meals can have in improving a player's performance.

Nutrition is your body's fuel. The primary goal of a good nutrition scheme is to keep your energy level as constant as possible, to avoid fatigue or other effects of too little or too much food.

One common misconception is that small meals or snacks are good for you. It is better to have fewer and larger meals and to avoid processed (refined) carbohydrates (sugar etc). Such habits will allow your body to better save and utilise the food's energy.

Johnny: 'Martin enjoys the balanced meals we eat as a family.'

Anne: 'Benjy had already been working on his fitness, but he wanted to make a change to his nutrition and start eating healthier to make the difference to his overall health. He spent a few months making healthier choices. Just before Christmas 2020, Benjy posted a picture of himself on Instagram and Twitter looking much leaner. In fact, he had lost 20kg in weight.'

HYDRATION

It is important to stay hydrated by drinking plenty of fluids before, during and after workouts, practice sessions or tournaments.

Keeping the body hydrated helps the heart pump blood more easily through the blood vessels to the muscles. Water is our life source. It makes up 70% of our body and is one of the best choices when it comes to meeting your body's need for fluids.

> **Drink water bro its hard op.**
> *Benjy*

> **Gonna start only drinking water from now on I think. Is it worth?**
> *Martin*

Martin raised money during the Twitch Rivals Community Charity Showdown in 2019, to help his charity Viva Con Agua pursue their vision to allow everyone in the world access to clean drinking water, hygiene facilities and basic sanitation.

Photo credit benjyfishy.

> **Posted on insta but thought would post on here aswell, 20 KG down :)**
> *Benjy*

Martin handing over the cheque of $125k to the founder of Viva Con Agua, Michael Fritz. Photo credit MrSavage.

GAMING BURNOUT

Professional Fortnite players tend to be a lot younger than most athletes with some players starting their careers in their early teens. At that age they do not necessarily have the experience to recognise the symptoms of fatigue and burnout in order to adjust their behaviour.

The pressure that players put themselves under to succeed is immense. Staying at a top competitive level is very demanding.

If Benjy and Martin decided certain activities such as sponsorship events, tournaments or traveling would have a detrimental effect on their health, they would be actively encouraged to turn them down.

SYMPTOMS OF BURNOUT

 Reduced performance.

 Mental and physical exhaustion.

 Lack of interest in previously enjoyable activities.

The most important preventive measure to avoid gaming burnout is simply to take care of your sleep. In addition, it is important to take time out from gaming and focus your attention on something else.

Grinding more is not necessarily better. If you find the right balance between a healthy set of activities, such as time with family and friends, your results will probably improve as a result.

Johnny in deep concentration, making breakfast for Martin at their Airbnb during Twitch Rivals in San Diego, September 2019. Photo credit Aaron Mendez Films.

INJURIES

Physical injuries in competitive sports are a common risk that every athlete, including esports players, must take into consideration. Players are prone to injuries that can limit their ability to perform, and in some cases, these injuries can stop them from gaming completely.

BACK PAIN

There is a lot of advice about the best sitting position or seating posture for gamers and which chairs are best. The first thing to be aware of, however, is that there is no such thing as a normal position, as humans are not built to sit for hours at a time.

There are some sitting positions that are recommended and it would be worth investing in a good chair, gaming monitor and a height adjustable desk.

Johnny: 'Martin has a height adjustable desk and while he doesn't change height very often, it gives him a chance to easily adjust it when needed.'

Anne: 'Benjy has suffered from back problems in the past and he has found that when he got his new chair there was a significant improvement.'

Photo credit benjyfishy.

" **My herman miller chair came LETS GOOOOOOOOO!** "
Benjy

REPETITIVE STRAIN INJURY

In gaming one of the most common injuries is repetitive strain injuries (RSI). It is caused by hours of continuous gaming while performing the same hand motions repeatedly. For mouse and keyboard gamers, RSI typically occurs in the wrist, while controller players experience it more in their thumbs.

SYMPTOMS INCLUDE:

- Significant pain during and after activity.
- Local swelling and joint stiffness.
- Burning sensation.
- Aching pain.
- Pain lingers for extended periods of time.

Several top professional gamers in Fortnite have suffered from RSI including Benjy, David "Aqua" Wang and Cody "Clix" Conrod.

Anne: 'Benjy now sleeps with a wrist brace and does wrist exercises every day. He also got the help from Matt Hwu from 1HP (@HPforGamers) who looked at how he sits to come up with specific exercises and guidance.'

The photo below shows Benjy's right hand (his mouse hand) wrist angle was tilted almost 20 degrees to the right, away from a healthier neutral position. A more neutral position would also allow for more movement and flexibility, hopefully improving Benjy's gameplay.

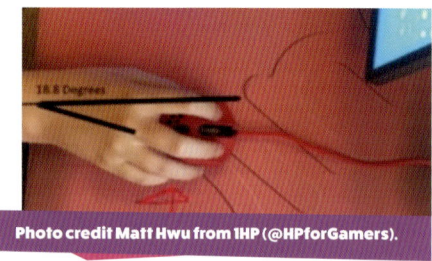

Photo credit Matt Hwu from 1HP (@HPforGamers).

SLEEPING POSITIONS

A sleeping position that is recommended for you can also improve your overall health.

Johnny: 'Martin has experienced shoulder problems in the past, this was because he was sleeping too much on his shoulder. His physical therapist recommended that Martin slept more on his back, which solved his problems after a couple of weeks.'

> **" I fell asleep on my right shoulder and now it hurts so much what do I do. "**
>
> *Martin*

EYESTRAIN

Eyestrain is caused by the small rapid eye movements and holding constant focus over time resulting in the muscles connected to your eyes to become irritated. The most common symptoms are fatigue, pain, blurred vision and headaches. Dry eyes are also a symptom showing itself through stinging or burning, sensitivity to light, redness or straining night-time vision.

To prevent eyestrain you should take breaks regularly. Try eye movement exercises such as to blink and hold eyes shut ideally every 5–10 minutes, looking at something far away.

Headaches can also be caused when your eyesight naturally becomes nearsighted or farsighted.

Both Benjy and Martin have their eyes checked by an optician every year.

TAKE ACTIVE BREAKS

It is important to get up from your chair and move around, ideally every 15–20 minutes or between each Fortnite match. Include eye, head, finger and arm movements in addition to moving around.

Benjy at his desk at home, July 2021.
Photo credit Emily Mudie Photography.

ESPORTS CAREERS

Whilst very few gamers actually succeed in becoming a professional player, esports offers many other career opportunities within the wider infrastructure.

Technology plays a huge role in business, meaning the skills acquired from gaming are easily transferable to careers outside of esports.

ESPORTS CAREER PATHWAYS

As the industry continues to grow around the world, more jobs and career pathways are being created in esports, creating a demand for people with specific skills.

TRANSFERABLE SKILLS DEVELOPED THROUGH PARTICIPATION IN ESPORTS

Teamwork | Leadership | Communication | Strategic Thinking | Problem Solving | Decision Making
Analytical Skills | Cyber Skills | Ability to Multi-task | Dexterity | Improving Processing Ability and Reaction Times

ROLES IN ESPORTS

Professional Player
Coach
Shoutcaster / Host
Analyst
Journalist
Observer
Admin Referee
Broadcast Production
Community
Social Media Manager
Team Player
Management and Operations
Streamer
Influencer
Video Editor
Photographer

ACADEMIC LINKS

Computer Science
Information and Communications Technology (ICT)

Sciences
Technology
Engineering
Mathematics
Creative Marketing
Business Studies
Entrepreneurship
Games Development
Sport

CAREERS IN TECH / DIGITAL / STEM INDUSTRIES

Cyber Security
Software Development
Big Data and Analytics
Cloud Solutions
Network Engineering
Mobile Technologies
Digital Engineering
Artificial Intelligence
UI / UX Design
Network Management
Virtual Reality
Software Engineering

GENERAL ROLES

Marketing | Sales | Advertising | Public Relations (PR) | Branding | Merchandising
Media | Event Management | Social Media | Design | Business Development

Source: British Esports Association and Pearson.

FINDING A JOB

If you are looking for a career within either esports or video gaming, it is not enough to just have a passion for the industry. Hiring managers are looking for those who have the right skill sets and experience as the main criteria; knowledge of esports comes secondary.

THE TOP HIRING SECTORS WITHIN ESPORTS:

- Marketing
- Business Development and Sales
- Software Engineering
- Executive and Management
- Social Media

THE TOP HIRING SECTORS WITHIN GAMING:

- Art and Animation
- Game Development and Design
- Quality Assurance/Games Testing
- Marketing
- Executive and Management
- Software and App Development

The esports job site Hitmarker has some helpful tips for getting your gaming career off the ground.

HITMARKER

Hitmarker is the largest gaming and esports job platform in the world as of 2021. It has over 12,000 active listings from more than 50 countries.

The company was founded in 2017 to fill a gap in the market as there was no specific website focusing on esports jobs. In March 2020, they expanded into the wider video game industry after finding that no platform was providing coverage of all available jobs there.

TOP TIPS FROM HITMARKER

1 Hone skills related to your core strengths.

2 Explore opportunities close to where you live.

3 Spend time perfecting your resume and cover letter.

4 Be proactive in your spare time.

5 Utilise social media and be visible.

6 Attend tournaments and events.

7 Consider volunteering to gain valuable experience.

How do you turn the above advice into practical steps to help you get hired? First, consider taking some actions to sharpen the hard skills you will need for your chosen speciality, such as a Google certification or online course in your field.

Build your social media presence. You will be able to find opportunities in your local area, as well as engage meaningfully with relevant companies and organisations. Keep your social feeds 'on-brand' and free of toxicity.

Make sure your CV or resume is polished and up to date. Bonus points if you customise it for every job you apply for. Similarly, write a unique cover letter for each application, tailored to the job and company.

Networking is key. Use social media, as well as online and live events, to meet influencers and company representatives in your sector. Make a good impression and you will be remembered.

Volunteering can be a great way to boost your CV or resume if you do not have a lot of work experience. Get involved with local tournaments and other events.

For more support and guidance as you search for your dream esports job go to Hitmarker.net.

The Hitmarker section on this page has been written by Trevor Harwood, Will Whittingham, Cam Brierley and Thomas Jeffery.

INTERNSHIPS

Internships are offered year-round and are a great way to gain experience within the industry. Most start each year for the summer period. It's mainly the larger companies that post these, so that is who to keep an eye on.

Photo credit Laurie Munslow.

HITMARKER

Hitmarker is one of the largest gaming and esports jobs platforms in the world and has more than 12,000 active listings from more than 50 countries. Below is a comparison prepared by Hitmarker showing the growth of opportunities in the industry during 2018 and 2019.

ESPORTS JOBS IN 2019

■ 2018   ■ 2019   ⌒⌄ PROPORTION

LEVELS (EXPERIENCE)

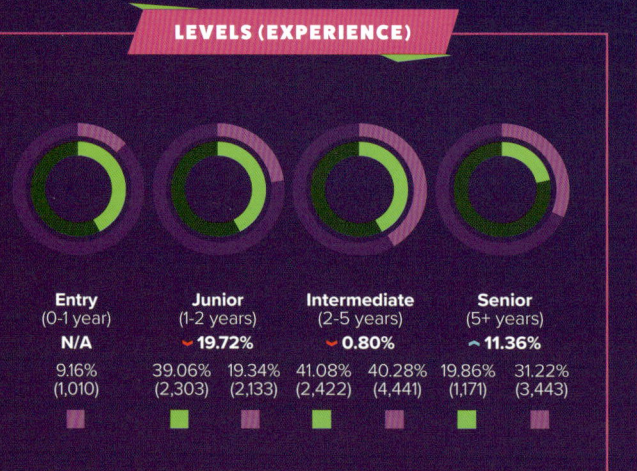

Entry (0-1 year)	Junior (1-2 years)	Intermediate (2-5 years)	Senior (5+ years)
N/A	⌄ 19.72%	⌄ 0.80%	⌒ 11.36%
9.16% (1,010)	39.06% (2,303) 19.34% (2,133)	41.08% (2,422) 40.28% (4,441)	19.86% (1,171) 31.22% (3,443)

COUNTRIES

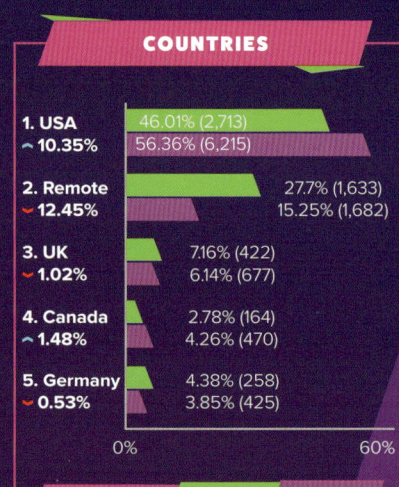

1. USA
⌒ 10.35%
46.01% (2,713)
56.36% (6,215)

2. Remote
⌄ 12.45%
27.7% (1,633)
15.25% (1,682)

3. UK
⌄ 1.02%
7.16% (422)
6.14% (677)

4. Canada
⌒ 1.48%
2.78% (164)
4.26% (470)

5. Germany
⌄ 0.53%
4.38% (258)
3.85% (425)

0% — 60%

#Job postings: 2018: 45   2019: 53

SECTORS

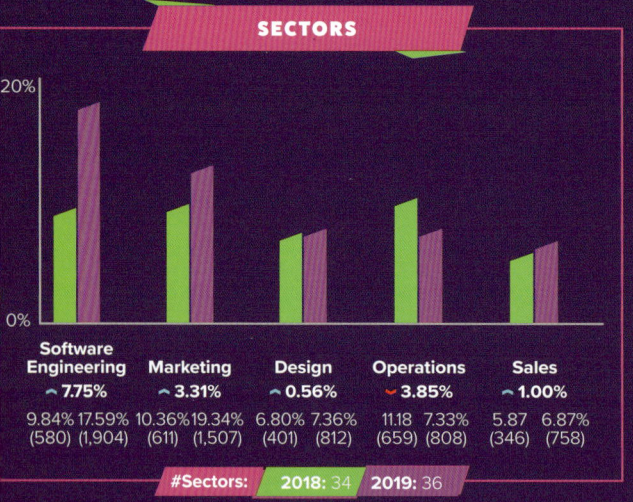

20%

0%

Software Engineering	Marketing	Design	Operations	Sales
⌒ 7.75%	⌒ 3.31%	⌒ 0.56%	⌄ 3.85%	⌒ 1.00%
9.84% 17.59% (580) (1,904)	10.36% 19.34% (611) (1,507)	6.80% 7.36% (401) (812)	11.18 7.33% (659) (808)	5.87 6.87% (346) (758)

#Sectors: 2018: 34   2019: 36

COMPANIES

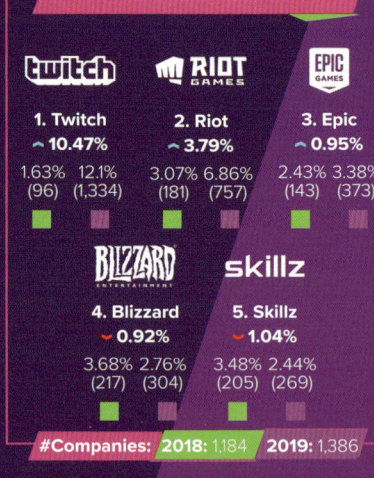

1. Twitch
⌒ 10.47%
1.63% 12.1% (96) (1,334)

2. Riot
⌒ 3.79%
3.07% 6.86% (181) (757)

3. Epic
⌒ 0.95%
2.43% 3.38% (143) (373)

4. Blizzard
⌄ 0.92%
3.68% 2.76% (217) (304)

5. Skillz
⌄ 1.04%
3.48% 2.44% (205) (269)

#Companies: 2018: 1,184   2019: 1,386

STATES

4000 ──────────────────────────── 0

1. California	2. Washington	3. New York	4. N. Carolina	5. Georgia
⌃ 4.1%	⌃ 0.17%	⌄ 1.62%	⌃ 1.4%	⌄ 0.17%
59.34% 63.44%	6.56% 6.73%	7.51% 5.89%	2.83% 4.23%	3.24% 3.07%
(1,610) (3,943)	(178) (418)	(204) (366)	(77) (263)	(88) (191)

#States: **2018:** 42   **2019:** 44

CONTRACTS

80%

0%

Full time	Part time	Freelance	Internship	Volunteer
⌃ 10.73%	⌄ 0.94%	⌃ 0.87%	⌄ 1.63%	⌄ 8.30%
64.81% 75.54%	4.22% 3.28%	6.85% 7.72%	5.95% 4.32%	18.18% 6.87%
(3,821) (8330)	(249) (362)	(404) (851)	(351) (476)	(1,072) (1,089)

PAID / UNPAID

■ Paid	■ Unpaid	■ Paid	■ Unpaid
77.87%	22.13%	88.01%	11.99%
(4,591)	(1,305)	(9,705)	(1,322)

PAID ⌃ 10.14%

TOTALS

5,896

⌃ 87.03%

11,027

Ballatw (right) at ESL Katowice Royale in 2019 together with Jason Kaplan. Photo credit Ballatw.

BALLATW

Arten "Ballatw" Esa is a streamer, caster, educator and analyst

Ballatw (pronounced 'Balla') is very respected in the Fortnite casting scene, known for commentating the 2019 Fortnite World Cup finals and DreamHack Anaheim 2020, and other major events like FNCS.

WHAT IS YOUR BACKGROUND IN ESPORTS?

Ballatw: 'Almost every summer I would casually play on random CS teams. In 2017 I took it seriously, trying to bring a team of young players up to the highest level as an in-game leader. When I got married, I returned to playing for fun and every once in a while casted the games of those guys. By that point we were really bored of CS:GO, it wasn't as fun so we decided to play some games and Fortnite was the first one we tried.

I started to play competitively and started making content, knowing that I would love to work on an analyst desk. I wanted the pro scene to respect what I said and I wanted to create useful content for both them and others.'

HOW WOULD YOU EXPLAIN WHAT YOU DO AS AN EDUCATOR AND ANALYST?

Ballatw: 'I make educational content to help all tiers of Fortnite. I teach the game by watching pros play and analysing what they do. I worked with a lot of the major practice discords to create pathways to play with the best players. The biggest gap here was tools as there was nothing really to determine who was good in these games. I worked with a few different developers to try to come up with solutions for this.'

HOW WOULD YOU EXPLAIN WHAT CASTING IS ALL ABOUT?

Ballatw: 'Casting or commentating simply contextualises what the viewers are watching and helps them understand the moment they are witnessing. It's a way to add emotion and narrative that connects and entertains viewers. A caster requires knowledge of the players participating and a skill in presenting this knowledge with humour, word choice, rhythm and intonation.'

HOW DID YOU GET INVOLVED IN FORTNITE'S OFFICIAL BROADCASTS?

Ballatw: 'When I went full time in 2019, I worked hard on my content and tried to establish connections. I actually DM'ed (direct messaged) my connections and said I would love to be involved in any capacity possible. There weren't very many casters back then so I knew that Epic Games were actively looking for people for Fortnite. It turned out that my content had already been noticed, and their producer was already working to reach out to me.'

WHAT HAS BEEN YOUR FAVOURITE TOURNAMENT TO CAST?

Ballatw: 'I got to cast on a stage with a high tier production team and an audience (albeit small) for the first time at ESL Katowice Royale in 2019. In my opinion, TwitchCon Twitch Rivals in San Diego definitely had the best audience that Fortnite has ever seen, the Aydan vs Martin 1v1 in game two of the finals was a crazy moment! Then last has to be DreamHack Anaheim in 2020. I will always cherish the fact that the players really bought into our makeshift production and broadcast, and sat down with us between games and after long days. It was awesome.'

 HOW DO YOU MANAGE TO CAST A GAME WITH A LARGE NUMBER OF TEAMS AND PLAYERS LIKE IN TRIOS?

Ballatw: 'It's not easy to have that knowledge of every team and their history and be able to draw on it during every moment. You have to keep track of the match status and every team's status. One way I do this is by trying to put them in buckets of 'relevant' teams. While every team is important, those who have a chance at winning the tournament are that much more important. So I keep tabs on them, their position, if all their players are alive. Then the standings come into play as well, knowing the format and what is achievable in one game. It's really hard but it's important that we are trying to predict what happens next. The really great thing about trios is that it is only 33 entities and I can think of teams as one rather than 3 players.'

 WHAT DO YOU NEED TO DO TO BECOME A SUCCESSFUL CASTER?

Ballatw: 'Know how to cast, know the right people and get noticed by the community you want to cast in. A caster should really get to know the technical side of broadcasts, especially audio. Get to know how the graphics works, how the switching is working in production, how the observing flow works — that all sounds very basic but understanding it helps you when you are casting for sure.'

 YOU HAVE INTERVIEWED BOTH BENJY AND MARTIN, HOW WOULD YOU DESCRIBE THEM AS PLAYERS AND AS A DUO?

Ballatw: 'They've both gotten so much more confident. I'd definitely say Benjy is humble and he doesn't like to brag, he is committed and fiercely focused on the tasks at hand. When I interviewed him at DreamHack Anaheim in 2020, I definitely could feel how the entire time he was thinking about the next step in his game. Martin is actually similar, he's a bit more outgoing, but not by much. It feels like he's always deep in his thoughts and it seems like he's very patient, but again, immensely competitive. They've got it all as a duo! They are comfortable with each other in all aspects, joking with each other and jovial. They can easily bring each other up after a disappointment and are always on the same page.'

 UNDERSTANDING COMPETITIVE FORTNITE CAN OFTEN BE HARD TO GRASP FOR A PARENT OR A RELATIVE OF AN ASPIRING PROFESSIONAL PLAYER SO HOW WOULD YOU EXPLAIN IT?

Ballatw: 'The first place to start is the basic concept — it's a battle of survival. In a Battle Royale, the last person alive wins and you earn points from being as close as possible to the last person alive, and also from eliminating others on your way there. Then when they look at the game mechanics, they might think it is very random in the way the circle moves, how loot drops and how players move. That's where I liken it to a game like poker — it's all probability. You want to maximise your probabilities to be favourable for you and when they aren't, do the best you can with a given hand.

Anything a player does is not random: the way they move, the way they loot, who they decide to shoot at is all trying to optimise how to survive.'

WHAT WOULD YOU SAY ARE THE MAIN CHALLENGES FOR YOUNGER PLAYERS AND THEIR PARENTS?

Ballatw: 'I think understanding is always the biggest challenge as it's really hard in a culture that still doesn't accept gaming as a healthy hobby. I think that some parents really aren't going through the effort to try to understand, simply because of the way it was for them growing up. However, even without understanding there can still be support, simply by communication. A parent telling their kid 'I support this and I will help in any way I can, even if I don't get it' can go a long way. Making it comfortable for kids to talk to others about it is important. Positive reinforcement goes a long way, but how is dad supposed to know you got third place in the tournament if they never made the kid comfortable to tell him in the first place. Trying to remove embarrassment is, at least

in my experience, what I would have wanted if I was doing this all over again.'

 IT SEEMS YOU HAVE A BIG HEART FOR ASPIRING PROFESSIONAL PLAYERS. WHAT IS YOUR BEST ADVICE TO THEM?

Ballatw: 'Some of my best skills in life come from my time competing. I've learned how to effectively communicate, be a leader, to listen, and other skills, which have helped me in engineering, in college, in marriage! So compete and learn from it! My other advice is don't focus on one avenue, work on the brand and be active in the public sphere, but don't do it all in one place. Use every platform available to you to grow your brand. In order to do this, use your networks, resources and support groups. If you need to do something feel free to ask them for help.'

Martin being interviewed by Ballatw in between matches at the DreamHack Anaheim Fortnite tournament in February 2020. Photo credit 100 Thieves.

INTERVIEW WITH
SHAUN "AUSSIEANTICS" COCHRANA

Streamer, caster (commentator), analyst and YouTube personality

AussieAntics mostly covers competitive Fortnite, and in November 2018 he started streaming on Twitch on a regular basis from his home in Sydney, Australia. He has casted events like the Australian Open Summer Smash 2020 and several Fortnite Champion Series (FNCS). We spoke to him about his work as a commentator and content creator within Fortnite prior to joining NRG in September 2021.

HOW DID YOU DECIDE ON THE NAME AUSSIEANTICS?

AussieAntics: 'I always wanted something that would have Australia or Aussie in it as I am proud of my heritage, but didn't want it to be tied to just gaming. I was always very conscious that one day my brand and content could expand and wanted to make sure my name was not tied to one title or even one genre of content.'

WHAT MADE YOU WANT TO GET INVOLVED IN ESPORTS COMMENTARY?

AussieAntics: 'I absolutely loved esports but have never found myself wanting to compete that badly due to other life commitments. I got involved in esports quite late but realised that even though I wasn't going to compete I could still be involved, as I had the potential to cast the game and create content surrounding it. I absolutely love it and take a lot of personal pride to do justice to the players.'

WHEN DID YOU START CASTING?

AussieAntics: 'In the early days, I was heavily involved in running the Fortnite practice scene in the Oceania (OCE) region, from hosting customs and scrims to putting on

my own tournaments that I funded myself and found sponsors for. I then began to do viewing parties and I would practise my commentary and found it got a really good response from the community.'

WHAT QUALITIES DO YOU THINK ARE NEEDED TO BE A SUCCESSFUL CASTER AND CONTENT CREATOR?

AussieAntics: 'I believe you need to have a love and passion for the title you cast; you need to know everything about the game and the players. On top of that, you obviously need the skills associated with casting: being able to articulate well, build up story lines, portray your emotion in your voice etc. For the content creation, you should find your own specific style and develop it to the fullest.'

WHY DID YOU CHOOSE FORTNITE AND WOULD YOU CONSIDER MOVING ON TO ANOTHER GAME?

AussieAntics: 'I have been playing games since I was three years old but always find myself fully investing in one game and one title and really embracing it. Fortnite is such a unique and interesting game that it has held my attention by far the longest. Now I am a public figure in the scene and absolutely loving every element of what I do. I can't see myself moving on for quite a long time.'

Photo credit **AussieAntics.**

181

WHAT HAS BEEN YOUR FAVOURITE TOURNAMENT TO CAST?

AussieAntics: 'This is a tough one, but the Australian Open 2020 is pretty hard to beat. Having a crowd, meeting all the players and getting to cast the winning game for one of my friends (Leevi "Breso" Breslin) who won $100,000, knowing how much it must have meant to him, was pretty special.'

THERE ARE NOT MANY CASTERS IN THE OCE REGION, DO YOU THINK THAT HAS HELPED YOUR CAREER?

AussieAntics: 'It has its advantages and disadvantages. It means that anything Fortnite related I am the go-to, but I have been able to branch into other titles due to the weight that it holds.

It is difficult here to make a living off just casting, so the fact I can couple it with content gives me the flexibility to not have to chase after every single opportunity. Being an Australian helps me be more recognisable as I stand out from a predominantly North America (NA) based team of casters.'

HOW DO YOU FIND THE PRESSURE TO CONSTANTLY BE CREATING CONTENT TO SUSTAIN AN INCOME?

AussieAntics: 'In the early stages I felt immense pressure to try and make my dream work. I always worked my other full-time job on top to make sure I sustained that income before taking the dive into full-time content creation. I have been on a constant upwards trajectory for over a year now, so I haven't dealt with the pressures of seeing things go backwards. It is a sad reality that content can be difficult to make a living in, but once you break into that upper echelon it changes dramatically. I am now just being as smart as I can and investing so I can set myself up while times are good.'

HOW DID YOU GET INVOLVED IN FORTNITE'S OFFICIAL BROADCASTS?

AussieAntics: 'Casting the Australian Open and a few other Fortnite events helped get my name out there, as well as building up a following and making casting content. When the official casters put on their own broadcast during squad FNCS I was called in which helped get me recognised.'

AussieAntics casting at the Australian Open 2020 together with Jon Kefaloukos (left). Photo credit Tennis Australia.

STREAMING AND CONTENT CREATION CAN BE ALL CONSUMING, SO DO YOU HAVE A TEAM TO HELP YOU?

AussieAntics: 'I have found especially recently that I have needed to develop a team of people around me to take some of the pressure and responsibility off. I have an editor and thumbnail designer who help me put out a video on my main channel seven days a week.

I have my second channel Extra Antics where I post short videos and fully edited highlight videos, so for that I have one of my mods who I also pay as my assistant to completely handle that. I am also signed to Click Management, a talent agency who handle all my endorsements and brand deals and that side of things.'

ARE YOUR PARENTS AND PARTNER SUPPORTIVE?

AussieAntics: 'Very. I am blessed to have parents who always supported me as I was not a very social kid and liked a lot of time to myself. When I wanted to make gaming a career, I kept my full-time job going on top and that showed just how badly I wanted it.

When I went full-time, they were sceptical, but they always supported and trusted me. I am also incredibly blessed to have a partner so supportive of my passion. She brings me back into reality sometimes when I haven't left my house in two weeks.'

WHERE DO YOU SEE YOURSELF IN TEN YEARS' TIME?

AussieAntics: 'Exactly as I do now, making content and casting. I love video games and esports so I wouldn't want to be doing anything else.'

WOULD YOU EVER CONSIDER MOVING TO THE USA?

AussieAntics: 'I have considered it quite a lot as the USA obviously has more shows and gives me reach to the EU as well. I would love to find a way to make it work.'

WHAT ADVICE WOULD YOU GIVE TO SOMEONE STARTING OUT?

AussieAntics: 'Find your niche. Take advice from others and model yourself on them but ultimately find something that makes you unique and attracts people to you specifically. Focus on improving your skills in the early stages and not the numbers. They will come.'

Photo credit AussieAntics.

BRENDAN "FALCONER" FALCONER

Professional player for 100 Thieves

Born in 1999, Falconer is one of the older Fortnite players on the professional scene. His most prominent achievement was his 5th place finish, with Diego "Arkhram" Lima, in the duos finals of the Fortnite World Cup 2019.

 HOW DID YOU BECOME A PROFESSIONAL PLAYER?

Falconer: 'I grew up playing football (soccer) competitively, but all of my free time was spent gaming. I never really considered myself good enough to be a pro in any games until Fortnite came along. 100T Arkhram and I got first place in the first week of the World Cup qualifiers, and from there I definitely went from a regular competitive player to pro status. Once I realised I just qualified for an insanely tough event, I knew I could classify myself as a pro player.'

From left to right: Arkhram, Falconer, Kyzui, Ceice, Klass. In front: Elevate. Photo credit @claudiopalma.

 DID YOU GET ANY SUPPORT FROM YOUR PARENTS ALONG THE WAY?

Falconer: 'My parents never liked the fact that I played so many games, but they never forced me to stop. Once I finally made it to New York and they saw the amount of people supporting me, they were glad they never interfered with the endless nights I would spend gaming because it finally paid off. My dad now helps me with contracts and sponsorships.'

 HOW DID YOU BALANCE YOUR PROFESSIONAL PLAYER CAREER WITH EDUCATION?

Falconer: 'In my first year I was doing a few college courses, but I realised that if I wanted to be as good as I could be, I needed to dedicate all the time possible to playing. A lot of people don't realise that the best players in the game are on the game more hours than they are asleep. It takes insane dedication to do that.'

 ARE YOU USING A FORTNITE COACH OR ANALYST?

Falconer: 'I am in a very smart friend group, so we learn and watch the game together.'

WHAT DOES A NORMAL DAY LOOK LIKE?

Falconer: 'My average day would be waking up around 1pm and I would be on my computer with other players from 3pm. We practise our mechanical skills and play each other in creative maps. For the last few weeks, I have been able to fit in gym time, so I get on Fortnite at 4pm and play all through the night and repeat the same schedule every day. In my spare time I hang out with friends occasionally doing outside activities, but it has gotten very minimal ever since I started taking Fortnite very seriously.'

DO YOU THINK SOME OF THE YOUNGER FORTNITE PLAYERS ARE RIGHT TO WORRY THAT THEIR REACTION TIMES WILL WORSEN AS THEY GROW OLDER?

Falconer: 'I don't think my reaction time is worse. I just think the interest is lost with people my age because they have other things to worry about. If I put in my max effort, I can keep up with a lot of the people I play with in my friend group, who I consider to be some of the top ten players worldwide. If you are my age, you are at a stage in life where if you don't see a complete, successful future, you either need to fully commit or start looking at opportunities outside of Fortnite. Players my age have moved on because of that reason. That's the beautiful thing about being a younger pro.'

WHERE DO YOU SEE YOURSELF IN THE FUTURE?

Falconer: 'I plan to eventually go back and get my business degree and then work in the esports business. I am blessed to be able to see how awesome 100 Thieves is from a business standpoint and in 3 – 5 years' time I see myself working for an organization like that.'

WHAT ADVICE WOULD YOU GIVE TO YOUNG TALENT WHO HAVE AMBITIONS TO BECOME A PROFESSIONAL PLAYER?

Falconer: 'Take small steps, try to get good by yourself and surround yourself with other people that try as hard as you do in the game. The most important part is to enjoy the game, because you will never be able to put genuine effort into something you don't love.'

Photo credit 100 Thieves.

SOCIAL MEDIA

The stereotype of a video gamer as an anti-social introvert seems very out-dated in the modern world. In fact, the esports community is very sociable and when players are not playing games, they are usually talking about them with each other, either IRL or on social media and messaging services.

Digital technology in the twenty-first century has made communication easier, faster and more accessible than ever before. Multiplayer games alongside social networking allow players to share their passion as well as connect to their friends online.

SOCIAL MEDIA PLATFORMS

There are multiple platforms that professional players can use to raise their social profile and connect with others.

TWITTER

Twitter allows people to send and receive short posts called Tweets. Benjy has been very active on Twitter, posting almost daily in periods and engaging with likes and replies. Martin has a slightly different approach to Twitter, as he posts and engages less. He says he does not want to spam his followers with too much content. Both Benjy and Martin's Twitter engagement work well, as they independently surpassed 1 million followers by January 2020. They use the platform in an authentic way and their Tweets reflect their individual personalities.

In the first half of 2020, there was more than 1 billion Tweets about gaming and Fortnite was the fifth most tweeted game in the world that year.

The so-called Engagement Rate is calculated by dividing the number of engagements (likes, Retweets etc) by the number of impressions (the number of times the Tweet has been seen). The ideal Tweet will have both a high impression number and a high engagement rate.

Creating Tweets that get a high engagement rate and build a loyal fan base is a skill. NRG signed @beehhive as their Executive Tweeter. NRG Bee is known within the Fortnite community for his amusing "viral" Tweets.

THINK BEFORE YOU POST

Posting something online without thinking can ruin both your online reputation and career even years later.

Do not share anything inappropriate or harmful on social media that you would not want your teachers, family or future employers to see. Even if the post is deleted, people could have seen it and even taken a screen grab.

DISCORD

Discord is a group-chatting platform, originally built for gamers. Fortnite players use Discord to voice and video chat, as well as live stream games and other programs. Benjy and Martin first met in a Discord friend group, with Mongraal, Milan and a few others. They later moved on to create a larger group called "IT", which included well-known players like Bugha, Smeef, Aqua and Nyhrox, many of whom qualified for the 2019 Fortnite World Cup.

IT Group at Fortnite World Cup 2019.

Both Benjy and Martin have a community of thousands of core fans on their personal Discord servers, where they make announcements and post game clips. Their fans can also interact with others, find friends and teammates and even become moderators who monitor online activity.

INSTAGRAM

Instagram is a free photo and video sharing service where people can upload photos or videos and share them with their followers or with a select group of friends. Benjy and Martin started to use Instagram in 2019, mainly for posting short Fortnite clips, but also the occasional photo of themselves.

TIKTOK

TikTok is a social video sharing service that allows users to create short music, lip-sync, dance, comedy and talent videos of 3 to 15 seconds, and short looping videos of 3 to 60 seconds. Both Benjy and Martin started sharing Fortnite highlight clips in March 2020, with a steady increase in followers and viewership.

FOLLOWERS / SUBS

AUG 2021	MARTIN	BENJY
TWITTER	1.2M	1.7M
INSTAGRAM	2.7M	2.4M
TWITCH	2.3M	3.6M
YOUTUBE	1.8M	1.6M
TIKTOK	1.1M	1.2M

Martin celebrating 1 million followers on Instagram, July 2019. Photo credit MrSavage.

189

YOUTUBE

YouTube is a video sharing service where users can create their own profile, upload videos, watch, like and comment on other videos. Benjy and Martin edited and uploaded their first videos, which are still available to watch on their YouTube channels. Benjy published his first video in September 2018, while Martin's first video was in March 2018. Now Benjy and Martin both have editors who download their gameplay stream, collate the best clips and post a highlights video on YouTube. Sometimes they record their gameplay to disk instead of streaming and use the recordings as a source of content for their YouTube channels.

Martin has three YouTube channels. In addition to his main channel, he has a channel named "MrSavage RAW" which features full unedited games from his tournaments and a "MrSavage Shorts" channel which shows clips from his game play. Benjy also has a second channel for clips called "benjyfishy Shorts".

FUN FACT

Of Martin's top five most viewed YouTube videos per September 2021, three of those are with Benjy, all with more than 2.8 million views. This shows how enormously popular the duo is.

TWITCH

Twitch, the live streaming platform, is a great place for a player to share their gameplay with others. Successful streamers manage to engage the viewers as well as creating a space for friends and fans to meet and interact. Moderators help players by deleting any inappropriate, offensive messages or gamer tags that may appear during their stream.

Benjy and Martin started streaming their Fortnite gameplay to online viewers in 2018, however both of them seldom hit more

than ten viewers during the first few months. But it was a valuable time to practise in front of a live audience, before their viewership increased rapidly during late 2018 and early 2019. According to Twitch statistics service SullyGnome, during 2020 Benjy had about 22k average concurrent viewers while Martin had about 7.5k.

OTHER SOCIAL MEDIA PLATFORMS

Snapchat is a popular messaging app that allows users to exchange pictures and videos (called snaps). Since content is only available for a short time before becoming inaccessible, the platform has not lent itself to the type of content Benjy and Martin usually publish, therefore they do not use it.

Facebook is among the oldest and most well-known social networking services. Neither Benjy or Martin use this platform, however be aware that there are a couple of fake benjyfishy and MrSavage accounts that are updated regularly.

Reddit is a social news and discussion website. Neither Benjy nor Martin use the site however there is plenty of benjyfishy and MrSavage related discussion on there.

TOP TIPS

Know your audience. **1**

Share content that is relevant to your fans. **2**

Monitor the response, what worked or did not work. **3**

Repurpose popular memes and short videos with some humour. **4**

Understand the best practices of each platform. **5**

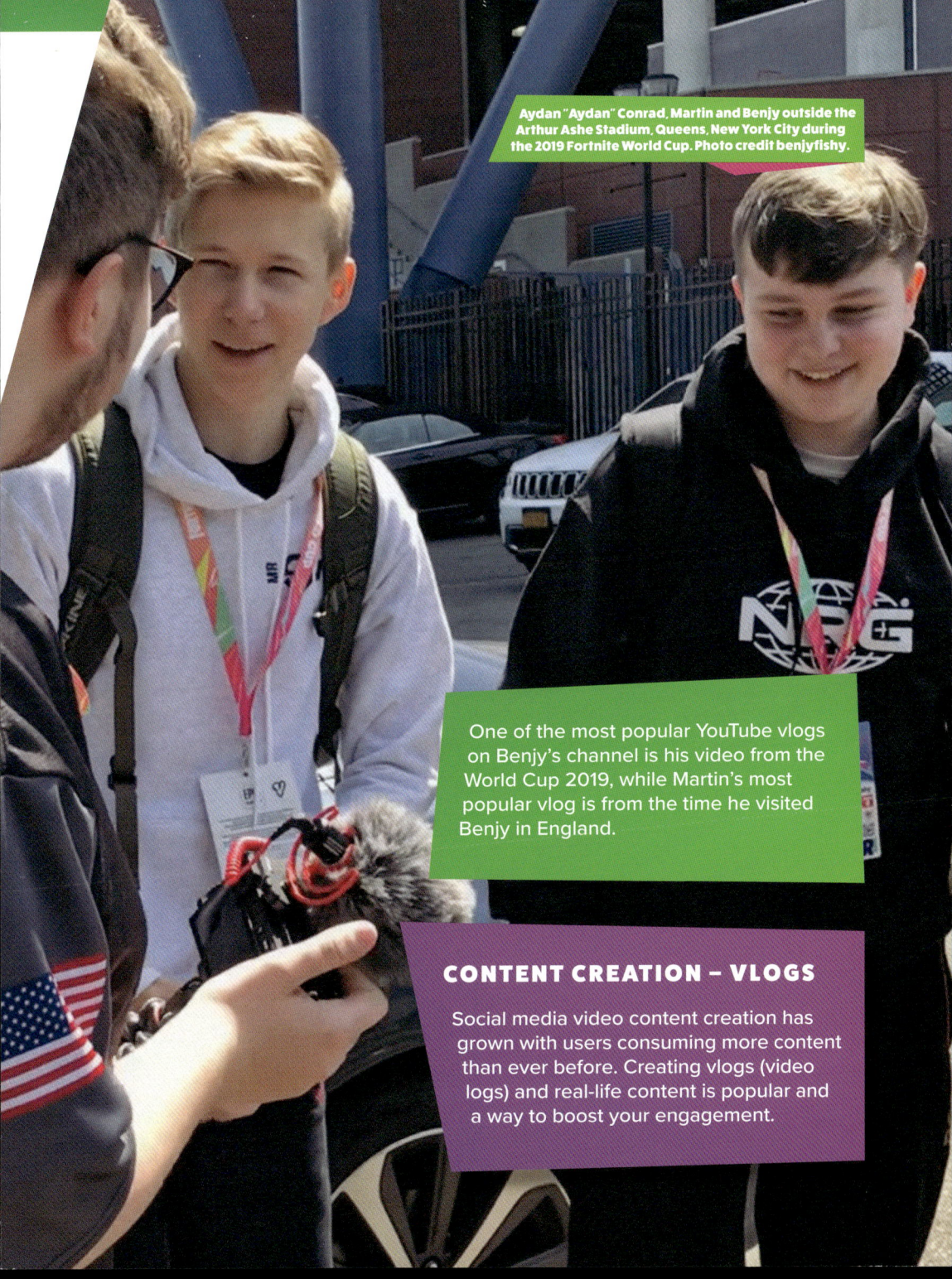

Aydan "Aydan" Conrad, Martin and Benjy outside the Arthur Ashe Stadium, Queens, New York City during the 2019 Fortnite World Cup. Photo credit benjyfishy.

One of the most popular YouTube vlogs on Benjy's channel is his video from the World Cup 2019, while Martin's most popular vlog is from the time he visited Benjy in England.

CONTENT CREATION – VLOGS

Social media video content creation has grown with users consuming more content than ever before. Creating vlogs (video logs) and real-life content is popular and a way to boost your engagement.

Q WHAT ARE THE MOST IMPORTANT THINGS TO LEARN TO BECOME A CONTENT CREATOR?

Grady: 'The most important thing to learn is that you have to start doing it. You have to just start creating. Your first idea is probably not going to go viral, but you'll learn. I have stuff out on the internet that is super cringe and missed the mark, but it got me to where I'm at today, where I feel like I have a strong handle on being able to make content that I think is good. I once was a kid looking for all the answers on YouTube on how to blow up, and I never found any good advice. The only thing that helped was just by starting to do it and paying attention to the other people who were doing it and seeing what worked for them and trying to figure out a way to do that for myself!'

GRADY RAINS

Castle Creator and Executive Producer at NRG
Esports and CEO at Full Squad Gaming

Grady brings his natural charisma, high energy and humour to all the content he produces. Grady has worked with both Benjy and Martin when he played an important role in igniting their social media presence early on in their careers. He is an endless source of creative ideas and is currently working on a lot of different initiatives, so we were glad he had the time to chat with us.

 YOU ARE A CASTLE CREATOR, AN EXECUTIVE PRODUCER AND RECENTLY A CEO. COULD YOU TELL US HOW YOU MANAGE ALL OF THESE ROLES?

Grady: 'Haha, yes I think I have the most confusing personal brand ever. It feels like I'm doing something new every day, but that's what I love about gaming! NRG basically has a small content team with a high output and I'm in charge of coming up with ideas and finding ways to make everything run smooth and efficient. I also specialise in a lot of the big organisational announcements and moments, as well as appearing in some of the content as a master of ceremonies (MC) or host. I worked with both Benjy and Martin a lot in 2019 and gave them tips on their content. Some of my first big videos were when we had Benjy and Martin meet up and we all posted a video at the same time on the same day.

My position as the Castle Creator falls in line more with being an MC or host. Originally, I was the construction project manager and had to oversee turning a warehouse into a fantasy factory. I hired a set designer and art director and had them help me brainstorm and oversee a construction crew that brought my dream into a reality. I think a lot of times the construction workers were pretty confused when they found out I was running the show!'

 WHAT IS THE NRG CONTENT CASTLE AND WHERE DID YOU GET THE INSPIRATION FOR IT?

Grady: 'The Content Castle is a 15,000 square foot, gaming fantasy factory in the heart of Los Angeles – it's like Willy Wonka's chocolate factory but for gaming. It's a permanent base for gaming influencer activation, and a studio for the creation and exploration of over the top and viral gaming content. It's also the HQ for NRG brands and home to our content universe.

We had gamers all over the planet playing for us and I realised that a lot of them like to have their own space. Instead of chasing them around the world to film, we could build a space in LA and it would be totally optimised for content. Gamers also don't turn into actors and comedians just because you put a camera on them. I wanted to create a space where they felt comfortable and there wasn't a ton of pressure for them to need to act or perform, but that they could just have fun and be themselves and the content would be able to create itself. My inspiration was Rob Dyrdek's Fantasy Factory MTV show.

Rob brought skateboarding to the mainstream through his set, where he decked out a factory into an indoor skatepark fun zone/office and celebrities would always stop by. I wanted to do the same for gaming so that celebrities and YouTube creators could visit, but it is definitely reserved for creators and not something that's just open to the public. At its core it really is a studio, so if you're not here to make content it's not exactly a theme park.'

WHAT IS FULL SQUAD GAMING COMPARED TO NRG?

Grady: 'Full Squad gaming is my latest project, where I am CEO. I wanted to launch a brand that bridged the gap between all the hardcore esports and gaming fans, and the other 2.7 billion gamers that call themselves gamers. I saw a huge open market for what I like to identify as the common gamer and wanted to create a brand separate from NRG to attack it.

It's all owned by the NRG people, so some people got confused that I left NRG, but it was basically just a cool way to start a new company under the same umbrella that is the NRG network.'

BOTH BENJY AND MARTIN ARE MAINLY COMPETITIVE BUT HAVE SPENT TIME ON CONTENT CREATION FROM THE START OF THEIR CAREERS. DO YOU THINK ALL COMPETITIVE PLAYERS SHOULD DO THAT?

Grady: 'Yes, any athlete should work on their personal brand. I think it is important to find a balance of content creation and competitive to have a holistic career, so that your personal brand and business isn't built on a single point of failure. You could be one meta change away from becoming competitively irrelevant and having a content creation bed to fall back on is always a good idea. However, some people just aren't passionate about it, and that's cool too! Do what makes you happy.

Players like Benjy and Martin have so much pressure on them. They are young, but luckily, they both seem to have a passion and love for content creation, and I think people can see how authentic it is and it will set them up really well for a long career.'

DO YOU DO ANY VIDEO FILMING AND EDITING YOURSELF? SHOULD EVERY CONTENT CREATOR LEARN EDITING AND FILMING?

Grady: 'I think it depends, but I did! Filming and editing yourself is a great way to learn what you want, what is possible with the software out there and will give you a good vision for your brand. Eventually someone else will oversee all of that, and sometimes the quicker you can get used to letting go control and having someone else do it the better. There's plenty of people who are excited to create content with talented people like Benjy and Martin, such as rockit (Benjy's editor) and Peter (Martin's manager).'

WHERE DO ALL YOUR IDEAS FOR THE VIDEO CLIPS COME FROM?

Grady: 'Ah jeez...I think to be a great creator you must be an avid consumer. There are no original ideas especially nowadays. I think more than anything it is about having a great taste and picking up on what people like and then recreating that in your own personal way.

I think my biggest tip for an aspiring creator would also be to not look at what the people who are huge are doing on these platforms, but to look at the people who are growing. Those are the people on the cutting edge and will help you develop your career.'

Q WHO ARE YOUR FAVOURITE CONTENT CREATORS?

Grady: 'Oh man, I like some weird ones! I like Asmongold because he is basically this dude who dedicated his whole life to World of Warcraft and has no regrets. He is just so incredibly authentic, and his persona cannot be duplicated because of the sheer number of hours he has put into it. I also love watching golf content on YouTube! The internet is such a niche place and I like to explore all the different communities and try to understand what makes them attractive to people. Sometimes I think I can get more insight on how a platform works out by watching random golf YouTube videos than a Ninja stream.'

Photo credit NRG.

NEGATIVE EFFECTS OF GAMING

While it is true that video games and esports have positive advantages, such as acquiring career and life skills as well as improving overall brain function, there is also a negative side. The most popular video games and apps are addictive by design, which can lead to gaming addiction. Other harmful online activities include cyber bullying and grooming.

In this chapter you will find out more about the negative effects of gaming, some tips and advice for both players and parents and where you can go to get more information and guidance.

GAMING ADDICTION

Out of the 2 billion people who play video games, the majority do not have an addiction to gaming. For most players, video games are a fun, relaxing and social activity – a way to connect with friends and enjoy a challenge. However for a few players it can turn into an addictive disorder that can take over their lives.

The World Health Organisation classifies addictive gaming behaviour as a "gaming disorder", in their International Classification of Diseases (ICD-11), which they claim affects only a small number of gamers. The difference between a healthy fun gaming hobby and an addiction is the negative impact the activity is having in your life.

WARNING SIGNS OF ADDICTION

 Isolating yourself from family and friends.

 Feeling upset and irritable when not playing video games.

 Avoiding activities that you once enjoyed.

 Skipping meals to focus on gaming.

 Disregard for basic things, like your personal hygiene.

 Tired and not getting enough sleep.

 Refusing to go to school and wanting to game instead.

 Playing in secret and hiding how many hours you play.

For parents, you should keep your eyes open and look out for any unusual behaviour in your child. Do not confuse healthy enthusiasm and enjoyment with a clinical disorder. If they show any signs that point towards addiction, you should talk to a professional.

THE PANDEMIC PROBLEM

During the COVID-19 pandemic there were extended periods of stay-at-home lockdowns, and as a result more children and parents became reliant on the Internet and digital devices to stay connected to the outside world. This became a vital tool for us to access learning, play, entertainment and social interaction, and the number of players gaming naturally increased.

The need to create a healthy balance between gaming and down time became even more crucial in households around the world.

SETTING BOUNDARIES AROUND GAMING

YoungMinds is a UK charity helping young people and their parents with their mental health. Their advice is:

 Enter into a family agreement to allow everyone in the family to negotiate screen limits together (ChildNet, a UK-based charity organisation with international reach has a template available on their website).

 Follow through on the consequences you have agreed.

 Think together about how to stop a gaming session. For example, stopping at the end of a particular level or time (be aware that some games including Fortnite cannot be stopped mid-game).

 Think about other offline activities that are enjoyable to do.

 Avoid arguments when emotions are running high.

FROM GAMING TO ESPORTS

A small percentage of players, such as Benjy and Martin, have a professional esports level gaming ability. In these cases, gaming activity will demand a lot more time and dedication than for most players. It is therefore even more critical, as with all top sports, that the player maintains a healthy balanced lifestyle (see the Keeping Healthy chapter, page 160).

On the way to becoming an esports professional, proving yourself as a player by displaying talent and gaining good results are key. Therefore communication at home is extremely important. Young players should try to educate their parents about esports in general and explain why practice is important ahead of competitions. Likewise, parents should take the time to understand their child's interest and be open to the fact that esports may offer a career opportunity.

If you believe that your gaming activity is becoming an addiction and is affecting your mental and physical health, ask for help.

Visit www.youngminds.org.uk for more information.

TEENAGE MENTAL HEALTH

Most people feel low or sad occasionally, this is a normal reaction to experiences that are stressful or upsetting. When these feelings continue over a period of time or take over and get in the way of your normal daily life, it can lead to someone feeling depressed.

Some signs of depression in young people include:

- Moodiness and irritability.
- Withdrawing from family, friends, and regular activities.
- Changes in sleeping and eating patterns.
- Fatigue and lack of energy.
- Difficulty concentrating.
- Tearfulness and frequent crying.
- Feeling guilty or bad, being self-blaming or self-critical.
- Thoughts of death or suicide.
- Feeling unhappy, miserable or lonely a lot of the time.

TALK TO SOMEONE

Sometimes the biggest hurdle is to admit to yourself that you need help and someone to chat or talk to, as there is unfortunately still a stigma associated with depression and mental health disorders. Irrespective of how small you think the problem is, thinking about it alone can often result in going in circles with no real progress, so it is important to be brave and take the first step.

Reaching out to your family or a trusted friend in the online gaming community may be a good place to start, as they might have experienced similar problems. However sometimes these problems might be too difficult for your friends or family to help with as much as they would like to. In this case, you might find a trained mental health professional or counsellor is a better support to you. There is a wealth of resources available online, but it may be hard to find the one you feel is right for you. We have included some as a starting point, see the green panel (next page).

CYBER BULLYING

Cyber bullying is bullying that takes place over digital devices such as mobile phones, computers and tablets. The most common places where cyber bullying occurs are:

- Social media (such as Facebook, Instagram, Snapchat and TikTok).
- Text messaging and messaging apps on mobile or tablet devices.
- Instant messaging, direct messaging, and online chatting over the Internet.
- Online forums, chat rooms, and message boards (such as Reddit).
- Email correspondence.
- Online gaming communities.

EXAMPLES OF CYBER BULLYING

 Sending unkind messages by email, text or instant messenger.

 Posting hurtful things about someone on social media.

 Spreading rumours or gossip about someone online.

 Making fun of someone in an online chat.

 Harassing or griefing someone in-game constantly and on purpose.

 Threatening someone online or in a message.

 Taking an embarrassing photo or video and sharing it without their permission.

ADVICE FOR PLAYERS

- Do not retaliate.
- Turn off the chat function.
- Mute or block other players.
- Leave and start another game.
- Report the bullying.
- Stop playing with people who bully others.
- Take a break for a while.

ADVICE FOR PARENTS

- If your child is being cyber bullied, offer comfort and support.
- Let your child know that it is not their fault, and that bullying says more about the bully than the victim.
- Praise your child for doing the right thing by talking to you about it. Remind your child that they are not alone.
- Reassure your child that you will work out a plan together to resolve this situation.
- Encourage your child not to respond to cyber bullying, because doing so just fuels the fire and makes the situation worse.
- You may want to take, save and print screenshots as evidence of cyber bullying.

#1 CHILDLINE 0800 1111
You can contact Childline about anything, whatever your worry. childline.org.uk

#2 NATIONAL BULLYING HELPLIINE
0845 22 55 787
nationalbullyinghelpline.co.uk

#3 STOPBULLYING.GOV
Free parent's helpline.
stopbullying.gov

#4 YOUNGMINDS
1-800-273-TALK (8255)
youngminds.org.uk

#5 SHOUT 85258
Text SHOUT to 85258 and chat by text

#6 THE MIX
themix.org.uk

#7 CHECKPOINT
Mental health resources for gamers and the gaming community.
checkpointorg.com

#8 MENTAL HEALTH AMERICA
mhanational.org

In the UK, you can report any concerns that you have about grooming or sexual abuse directly to the Child Exploitation and Online Protection Centre (CEOP). CEOP is part of the National Crime Agency and helps keep young people safe from online grooming.
www.ceop.police.uk/safety-centre

ONLINE GROOMING

Talking online is a great way to stay connected, and can often be a good way of making new friends. However it is really important to understand and be cautious of the dangers and risks of talking to someone online who you do not know.

Grooming is when a stranger seeks to build an online relationship with a young person, gain their trust and trick them in order to abuse or exploit them. This process can happen over a number of months or years.

The person will often:

- Pay compliments while playing the game or ask for tips or help with playing.
- Buy items for you in game.
- Ask personal or inappropriate questions.
- Ask to continue the conversation with you outside of the game.
- Try and show you that they have things in common.

TIPS FOR PLAYERS

 Never share personal information or photos with strangers online.

 Only chat online with people who you know in real life or who you have trusted friends in common with.

 Never agree to meet strangers from games in real life.

TIPS FOR PARENTS

 Observe your child's online behaviour and ask them who they have been communicating with.

 Set controls that prevent your child from accepting friend requests without your permission.

 Control privacy settings and make sure your child has private accounts.

 Make sure you know how to block other users and report suspicious activity.

" When Benjy first started gaming online and chatting with friends, I put the computer in a common area with the sound coming from external speakers as well as the headset so I could hear what the other players were saying to him. "

Anne

Photo credit Anne Fish.

ONLINE SECURITY

Online security is about protecting your personal and sensitive data from being misused by others on the Internet. There have been several incidents where top influencers and esports players have had their social media accounts compromised including Shroud, Bugha and Poach.

PASSWORD TIPS

- Create a strong password that has at least eight characters. The longer the better.
- Use a combination of both uppercase and lowercase letters, numbers and symbols.
- Do not include obvious personal information or common words.
- Do not recycle your passwords across websites and games.

SAFE GAMING

 Play only the authorised versions of games.

 Choose a username that does not reveal any personal information. Use unique passwords for every login.

 Make sure you have an updated antivirus or antispyware software installed and running on your computer. Some operating systems like Windows 10 will have preinstalled security software, which should be sufficient for most users.

 Verify the authenticity and security of downloaded files and new software by buying from reputable sources.

 Watch out for phishing, which is an attempt to obtain your information or data. Never click a link in an untrustworthy email or text message.

MULTI-FACTOR AUTHENTICATION (MFA)

One of the best ways to keep your accounts safe is to setup a multi-step authentication scheme, which requires users to verify their identities by providing multiple pieces of evidence before gaining access to a device, game or application.

The most common kind of MFA is two-factor authentication (2FA) which requires two different types of evidence. This includes two of something you know (password), something you are (fingerprint or face scan) or something you have (a secondary trusted device).

Benjy and Martin use two-factor authentication whenever available.

AUTHENTICATON APPS

Authentication apps generate security codes for signing into sites that require a high level of security. You can use these apps to get security codes even if you do not have an Internet connection or mobile service.

Some of the common authenticator apps are:

Google Authenticator

LastPass Authenticator

Microsoft Authenticator

Authy

sword

ONLINE SECURITY

PROTECTION

search?

DATA

Card

" As a parent, note that some games come with built in parental controls. Specifically, make sure to check out the parental controls in Fortnite, where you can control things around mature language, friend requests, name visibility and more. Fortnite also offers weekly playtime reports sent by email. "

Johnny

> **I used to play CS (Counter-Strike) so much. It was really bad. I would play like until 3am. Or I would go off at like midnight and then I would stay in bed until 3am watching Fortnite Moments videos. Then, I would wake up at 6am to go to school with like two hours sleep.**

Benjy

> **Going to bed at 7am sleep schedule is officially broken gn.**

> **I think i've got the god schedule now just woken up and its 6am good morning.**

Benjy

Photo credit Emily Mudie Photography.

NOCTURNAL LIFESTYLE

Getting the recommended amount of sleep can help teenagers maintain good physical health, emotional well-being and school performance.

The UK National Health Service (NHS) recommends that a teenager gets a minimum of 8 to 9 hours' sleep a night.

During adolescence the body's circadian rhythm (an internal biological clock) is reset telling a teenager to fall asleep later at night and wake up later in the morning.

This change has a strong tendency towards teenagers becoming more nocturnal, staying up later at night and sleeping longer into the morning.

Johnny: 'The Montessori school, which Martin attended, acknowledged the impact of the sleeping patterns of teenagers by allowing students in the lower secondary level to start school later in the morning than primary school pupils.'

Anne: 'For most of Benjy's teenage years he has lived nocturnally. Getting Benjy to go to bed and then waking him up in the morning has been a constant battle. During the school holidays Benjy would reverse his day and night, as he would be gaming all evening with his friends and then he would sleep most of the day.

Now that I have become more familiar with the esports world, I realise that this is a common lifestyle for most players, partly because most of the scrims and competitions take place in the evenings as well as the cross-region tournaments that the players compete in.'

Both Benjy and Martin manage to get the recommended amount of sleep, but they have shifted their timings, going to bed later and waking up later, keeping a consistent sleep schedule. They would fit studying and exercise around these timings.

LATE NIGHT TOURNAMENTS

Most practice scrims take place in the evenings as well as various online tournaments. When European (EU) players participate in cross-region events, they are often required to play in the early hours of the morning. For example the 2020 DreamHack online tournaments, in the North America East (NAE) Fortnite region, meant a 10 – 11pm start for EU participants. If the EU player got through to the finals they didn't finish until 6 – 7am in the morning.

In the EU Fortnite region, some Fortnite Champion Series (FNCS) games don't finish until around 10 – 11pm.

SLEEP TIPS

 Have at least 30 minutes of screen-free time before going to sleep.

 Cut out caffeine and energy drinks in the four hours before bed. Too much caffeine can stop you falling asleep.

 Do not binge eat before bed. A full stomach can lead to discomfort during the night and might prevent you sleeping.

 Try to keep a regular bedtime routine and create a good sleeping environment.

 Regular exercise helps you sleep more soundly. Aim for at least 60 minutes of exercise every day.

 Work with your parents – talk to them about the tournament times and come up with a plan of what you can participate in while keeping up with your studies.

REVENUE STREAMS

The growth of esports has seen a significant rise in revenue and prize pools for tournaments as well as sponsorship and media opportunities. Statista estimates the global esports market revenue will grow to an estimated $1.6 billion by 2024, up from $950 million in 2020.

Being signed by an esports organisation as a professional player or content creator is the equivalent of being signed by a top traditional sports team and with that comes high rewards. In this chapter we have explored the varied income streams that are available to professional players in esports.

The duo benjyfishy and MrSavage introduced during the 2019 Fortnite World Cup finals. Photo credit MrSavage.

EARNING MONEY FROM ESPORTS

In 2019, Epic Games announced that the Fortnite World Cup would offer a $30 million prize pool with a first prize of $3 million. This suddenly catapulted gaming and esports into the mainstream media, and during the finals in New York there were copious amounts of newspaper and TV coverage around the world. The public became more aware of what teenage gamers had known for a long time: that there were opportunities to earn significant money from gaming and esports.

Martin's 'No signal' hoodie. Photo credit Trygve Espejord.

ORGANISATION SALARIES

In the same way players and athletes earn wages in traditional sports; esports organisations pay their professional players a monthly salary. These can vary considerably, anything from a few dollars to $10k or more a month.

Salaries are based on a lot of different factors but are mainly focused around a player's tournament results and the size of their social media following. Most players act as brand ambassadors for their organisation, therefore a player who has a significant audience allows the organisation to establish larger marketing and sponsorship opportunities.

Players are often required to appear in brand campaigns including photo shoots, media appearances, social media posts and specific ads on their streams called overlays.

Some organisations may add additional monetary bonuses for hitting streaming targets such as a minimum of 40 or 80 hours per month. If you are signed as a content creator, such minimums will likely be higher. If you sign as a mainly competitive player, you need to make sure you do not over commit so that you have enough time to practise.

Always get any contracts looked at by a lawyer prior to signing. (See Support Team chapter, page 24)

SUPPORT-A-CREATOR CODE

Epic Games' Support-A-Creator program is a way for fans to support their favourite player or creator by entering the player's tag when they make a purchase in the in-game shops.

In Fortnite a player will receive USD $5 for every ten thousand V-Bucks (the Fortnite in-game currency) spent. Ten thousand V-Bucks amounts to about USD $100. The program was a very welcome initiative by Epic Games to help support gamers and content creators.

Payments are currently processed through Epic Games payment partner HyperWallet.

Epic Games' require that the hashtag 'ad' (advert) is clearly displayed after the player's tag. Benjy's tag is simply benjyfishy #ad while Martin's tag is 200IQ #ad.

HOW DOES THE REVENUE STREAM BREAK DOWN?

It is not all about prize money and there are other ways to earn an income from being a professional player or content creator, including:

Organisation salaries

Prize money

Streaming

YouTube

Sponsorships

Support-A-Creator Code

Merchandise and apparel

Donations

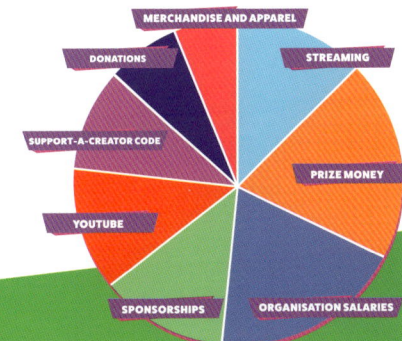

The illustration is included for graphical purposes only. The size of the slices does not reflect the actual relative size of Benjy and Martin's revenue streams.

From left to right: Fortnite World Cup 2019 top three: EpikWhale (3rd), Bugha (1st), psalm (2nd). Photo credit NRG.

BENJYFISHY

ONE MILLION SUBSCRIBERS

YOUTUBE

YouTube is a video sharing service where users can create their own profile, upload videos, watch, like and comment on other videos (see page 190).

Both Benjy and Martin have YouTube channels where they publish edited streams or recordings of their gameplay. Peter is responsible for Martin's channels (see interview with Peter, page 30). Benjy's channel is managed by his editor Henry "rockit" Orvis.

To earn money, you need to join YouTube's Partner programme, which allows you to monetise your videos. To qualify for the programme your channel must have at least 1k subscribers and 4k hours of accumulated watch time over the prior 12-month period*.

Direct costs associated with YouTube are mainly fees for video editing, making thumbnails and the process of publishing, which involves categorising and tagging the videos correctly. If you are partnered with a digital rights management vendor (to help with copyright issues and more) there will be additional commission to be paid.

PRIZE MONEY

Prize money is the most visible part of the boys' income and available online at sites like www.esportsearnings.com.

Most Fortnite tournaments are arranged by Epic Games, which is a US company. According to Epic Games' interpretation of US tax regulations, prize money is seen as a player's personal income. Therefore players cannot easily receive prize money through limited liability companies.

US residents are required to complete a W-9 form, while non-US residents must complete a W-8BEN form.

*As of January 2021.

TAX DEDUCTIONS

When Epic Games processes a prize payment, they withhold tax and send the amounts to the US Internal Revenue Service (IRS) on your behalf. The withholding rate for US residents is 24% and 30% for non-US residents*.

Each year Epic Games will submit figures to the IRS and you will receive a copy of a 1042-S form which shows the tax deductions.

If you are outside the USA, check with your accountant regarding the individual rules in respect of the US double taxation treaty and how that works within your country.

In the United Kingdom, it is possible to apply for a personal US ITIN (Individual Taxpayer Identification Number) via a Certified Acceptance Agent. You can reclaim the withholding tax on payments made in respect to non-US activities and declare revenue from US activities via the 1040-NR form.

Martin "behind the scenes" shooting a video for his personal sponsor ASUS ROG (Republic of Gamers) together with videophotographer Andreas Hem from Twins Productions. Photo credit MrSavage.

YouTube earnings vary depending on how many views you get per video, the time your viewers spend watching, and what ads are running. It can be anything from a few cents to several hundred dollars per video a month.

TWITCH AFFILIATE

Twitch is a live streaming service operated by Twitch Interactive, a subsidiary of Amazon. com, Inc (see page 190). Becoming part of Twitch's Affiliate programme allows qualified streamers to monetise their channel and build their audience, as they work towards becoming a Twitch Partner. The requirements to join the Affiliate Program are:

- Minimum 50 followers.
- Stream for 8 hours.
- Stream on 7 different days.
- Have an average of 3 viewers

You must simultaneously meet all four requirements over a 30-day period.

TWITCH PARTNER

Twitch Partners earn money just like Affiliates, but they also have other added bonuses, which can improve the quality of content or engagement with an audience.

To apply to become a Twitch Partner you need to have achieved the following:

- Stream for 25 hours.
- Stream on 12 different days.
- Have an average of 75 concurrent viewers.

Once you are able to apply, Twitch will manually review your channel to determine if you meet the requirements.

SUBSCRIPTIONS

Streamers earn revenue from viewers who subscribe monthly to their channel. Many people subscribe through the free subscription that comes with every Twitch Prime account. This is basically the same as a normal $4.99 per month so-called tier 1 subscription. There are also tier 2 and tier 3 subscriptions, which cost more per month. You will receive a percentage of each subscription. In May 2021 Twitch started making local variations in subscription pricing available in countries outside the US.

ADVERTISMENTS

Streamers earn a share of the revenue from any ads played on their channel. There is an option to control the frequency of ads in the Twitch dashboard, but Benjy and Martin do not use this automatic feature to avoid distracting their audience from enjoying their gameplay. Instead, they have chat moderators helping to run ads at more convenient times such as while they are waiting for the battle bus to launch.

MONETIZATION TOOLS

FEATURE	ALL STREAMERS	TWITCH AFFILIATE	TWITCH PARTNER
CHEERING WITH BITS	No	Yes No custom Cheermotes	Yes With custom Cheermotes
SUBSCRIPTIONS	No	Yes Up to 5 Unlockable Sub Emotes	Yes Up to 60 Unlockable Sub Emotes
ADS	No	Yes	Yes

VIDEO TOOLS

	ALL STREAMERS	TWITCH AFFILIATE	TWITCH PARTNER
TRANSCODING	As available	As available, with priority access	Full access to Transcode options
SQUAD STREAM	No	No	Yes
SUBSCRIBER STREAMS	No	Yes	Yes
VOD STORAGE	14 days	14 days	60 days
STREAM DELAY	No stream delay option	No stream delay option	Stream delay up to 15 minutes
RERUNS AND PREMIERES	No	Yes	Yes

DONATIONS

Viewers can hit a donation button to support a streamer. The typical donation is $1 but larger amounts like $5 or $10 are known to be donated from time to time.

A variety of third-party services exist to collect donations. Benjy and Martin both use Streamlabs who do not charge fees for each donation.

You can get payments paid into a PayPal account but there are fees associated with each transaction. Consider applying for PayPal's micropayment option, which keeps the fees on small transactions to a minimum.

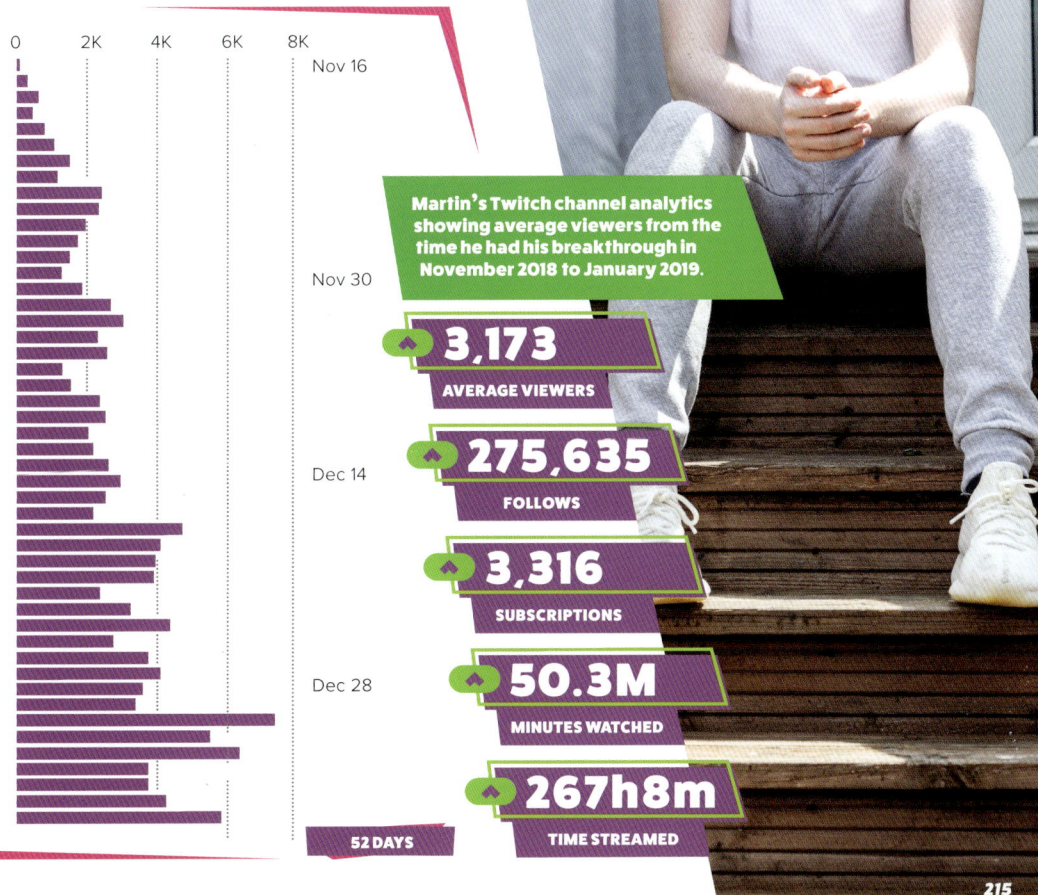

Photo credit Emily Mudie Photography.

Martin's Twitch channel analytics showing average viewers from the time he had his breakthrough in November 2018 to January 2019.

3,173
AVERAGE VIEWERS

275,635
FOLLOWS

3,316
SUBSCRIPTIONS

50.3M
MINUTES WATCHED

267h8m
TIME STREAMED

0   2K   4K   6K   8K

Nov 16

Nov 30

Dec 14

Dec 28

52 DAYS

PERSONAL SPONSORSHIPS

Esports organisations have their own sponsorship deals that they often require their roster of professional players to be involved in. However, depending on your contract there may be the opportunity for a player to have their own personal sponsors if they do not conflict.

Martin has ROCCAT, ASUS, KovaaK and Streamlabs as his personal sponsors. Photo credit MrSavage.

MERCHANDISE AND APPAREL

Martin has collaborated with a small Norwegian clothing brand, Calimera, mostly because he has an interest in apparel and wants his fans to have the opportunity to buy fanwear, and not so much for the income side. Martin's apparel is available for sale at mrsavage.gg/apparel, while Benjy's is still in development.

TRADEMARKS

Consider getting your name trademarked, which can be especially important if you plan to launch an apparel range or sell merchandise like drink bottles or stickers. Both Benjy and Martin have their names benjyfishy and MrSavage trademarked.

TIME-LIMITED CAMPAIGNS

Both Benjy and Martin work with agents who can bring in potential time-limited sponsorship campaigns.

These campaigns can be very lucrative, but usually come with short deadlines and specific last-minute requirements, which can often make it difficult to balance Benjy and Martin's practice and competitive schedules.

Nevertheless, Benjy and Martin have said yes to a few of these as most often these are brands that are connected directly to gaming, for example the Apex Legends Season 3 launch in September 2019 that was sponsored by Electronic Arts.

Long-term sponsorships are easier to schedule practice around while also providing a steady monthly income.

The motif on the back side of Martin's No signal hoodies. Photo credit Trygve Espejord.

Custom ELO headset made for Martin by ROCCAT. Photo credit MrSavage.

ELO

MR SAVAGE

HUNDRED THIEVES

Florian Herrmann at ROCCAT's marketing department in Germany discovered Martin's talent late in 2018. This led to a successful sponsorship deal as Martin has been using ROCCAT gear, like his headset, mouse and keyboard ever since.

ROCCAT

COALITION OF PARENTS IN ESPORTS

In 2020, a group of parents of professional players and recognised content creators from around the world worked together to create a non-profit organisation to encourage the positive aspects of healthy gaming.

Devin "Duster" Williams (@dusterfn), son of COPE co-founder Shae Williams (@Shaemmon). Photo credit Shae Williams.

COPE HISTORY

When Shae Williams (mother of Devin "Duster" Williams) and Dave Herzog (father of Jordan "Crimz" Herzog) realised that they had both, separately, been educating international players and their parents about esports, they decided it was time to join forces, work together and create a team to improve esports education while also dispelling negative misconceptions of gaming.

They partnered with esports college programmes and recruitment organisations, promoting team and scholarship opportunities, and have now worked with over 200 colleges in the USA. COPE support players and parents from around the world.

For more information vist: www.cope.gg

Henrik "Hen" Mclean – Guild Hen @hentvv.
Photo credit Guild Esports.

COPE SERVICES

This is just a selection of the services that COPE offer to gamers and their parents:

FOR GAMERS:

 A series of open tournaments with awards to promote fun competition and player recognition.

 Opportunities for mentorship with your favourite professional gamer.

 Resources to help you increase your competitive gaming skills.

 Resources and education to help you grow your brand.

 Tips to optimise your hardware and software technology.

 Information on leveraging your accomplishments on your college applications.

 Advice on how to keep your body and mind fit and healthy for best performance.

FOR PARENTS:

 Resources and education informing you on the safe and beneficial ways for your child to engage and grow in the world of online gaming, esports competition and content creation.

 General information and a place where any of your questions or concerns regarding esports will be answered.

 Opportunities for mentorship for both parents and gamers.

 A supportive community of other esports parents.

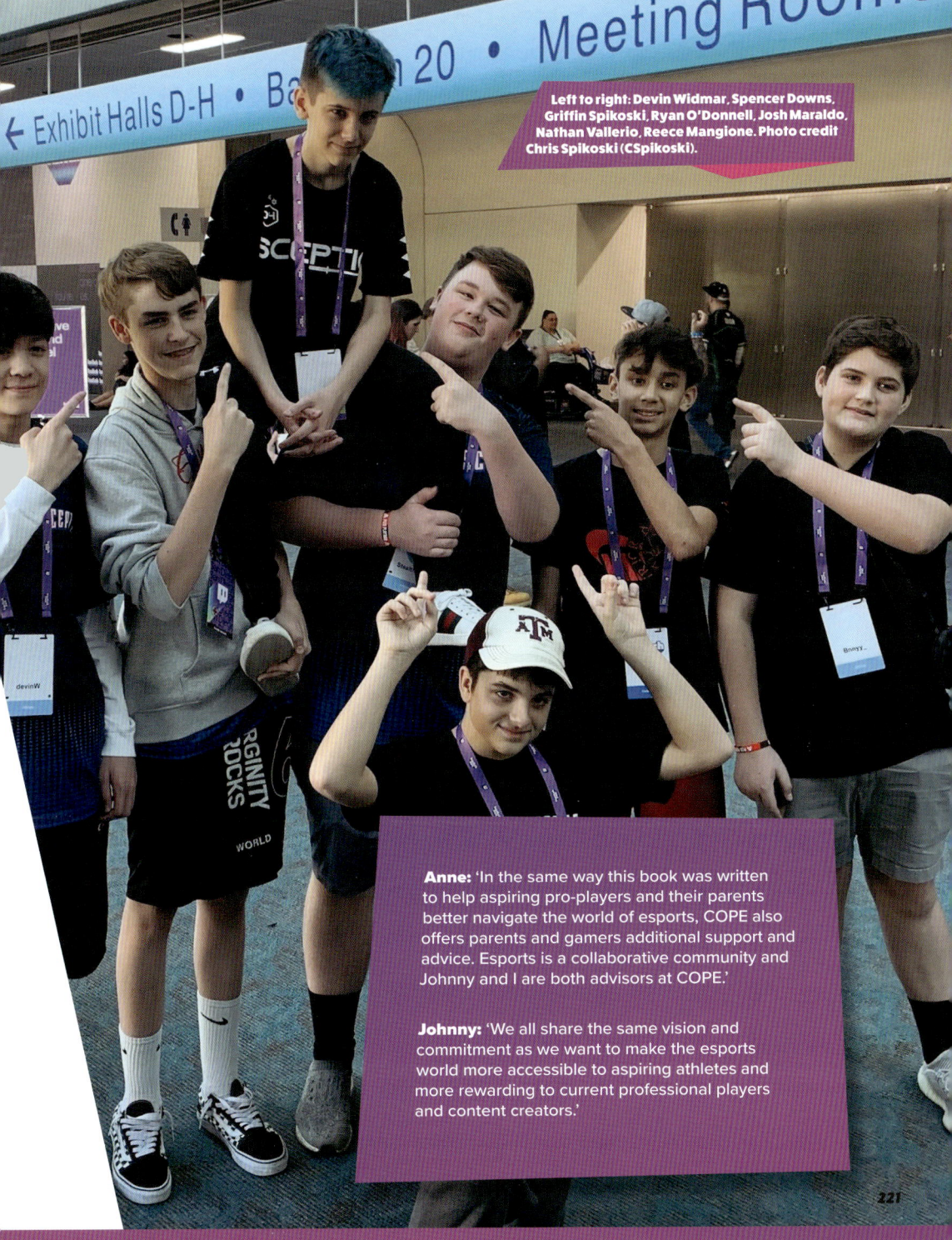

Left to right: Devin Widmar, Spencer Downs, Griffin Spikoski, Ryan O'Donnell, Josh Maraldo, Nathan Vallerio, Reece Mangione. Photo credit Chris Spikoski (CSpikoski).

Anne: 'In the same way this book was written to help aspiring pro-players and their parents better navigate the world of esports, COPE also offers parents and gamers additional support and advice. Esports is a collaborative community and Johnny and I are both advisors at COPE.'

Johnny: 'We all share the same vision and commitment as we want to make the esports world more accessible to aspiring athletes and more rewarding to current professional players and content creators.'

NOT OUR ENDGAME

The esports industry is rapidly developing and we only have just scratched the surface in this book, as we could have written so much more on each area. But we truly hope that by sharing our experience of supporting Benjy and Martin in their careers, and by imparting our advice we can help young aspiring professional players and their parents – as well as anyone else that would like to support players or understand more about competitive Fortnite and esports.

Both of us feel like we have much more to offer the esports community, so do not consider this to be the final words from us.

Anne will continue to help out Benjy in his career. She will carry on guiding the next generation by sharing her experience and knowledge live at twitch.tv/mamabenjyfishy1, through her blog articles on www.mamabenjyfishy.gg and her Tweets at twitter.com/mamabenjyfishy.

Johnny will continue to work with Martin's professional team and share his insight about esports and more on his blog www.deeperdown.com and through his Tweets at twitter.com/MrTroset.

Whatever you want to build in life – take it step by step. And if you want to build it like benjyfishy and MrSavage, we hope to have helped you along the way.

Enjoyed reading this book?
Tell us at buildit@mamabenjyfishy.gg or buildit@deeperdown.com.

THANK YOU

ANNE

I would like to dedicate this book to the memory of David, who is always in our hearts. Special thanks to Charles and my parents for all that you do.

Thanks to all my friends and fellow islanders in Sunbury-on-Thames, to Benjy's schools and to my work colleagues at CSL who have been a valued support through the years.

Special thanks to all of our friends in the esports community who we have met along this journey, to all at NRG for nurturing Benjy's talent, to Henry "rockit" Orvis and Brandon Freytag at Loaded.

Thank you to Johnny, Martin and family, your support and friendship has been invaluable and is testament to the camaraderie in the esports community. I am excited to see what the future brings.

JOHNNY

I would like to thank my mother Anne Mari for supporting my curiosity and interests early on, and my father Magnar for sharing his love for nature and always being proud of me. Special thanks to my wife Solfrid and my son Mikael for their support. To my brothers Gøran and Geir – I love you.

Special thanks to Martin's personal manager Peter Rudi Pettersen for always being creative, positive and a trusted support to Martin and myself. A special thanks also to Erik "Bloodx" Guttormsen for nurturing Martin's talent and assisting both him and me into the world of esports. Thanks to our agent and advisor Cengiz Tüylü for sharing his unique experience and insight in the business of esports, to Hugo Berg Otterlei for his insight in legal matters, and to Roberth Hansen, Teodor Thoresen Skarpaas and Marc Serra for their support.

It has been a pleasure to get to know Anne, Benjy and Charles along the way. Anne, your friendship, cooperation and support have been invaluable. I could not have done this without you. The race is long!

WE BOTH WOULD LIKE TO THANK

Benjy and Martin for allowing us to be part of their journey and sharing their stories.

Thanks to NRG and 100 Thieves for their continued cooperation and permission to use their photos.

Thanks to all involved in helping us produce this book, especially for the editorial feedback from Gemma Whelan, and book design from Callum Bowdler. Thanks for the involvement of COPE, Esports Healthcare, Pearson, Hitmarker, SpecialEffect, Confetti Institute of Creative Technologies, Staffordshire University, NCSA and the British Esports Association.

Thanks to everyone else that provided feedback. Special thanks to all that participated in our interviews and answered our questions. There is not room to thank you all by name, but your effort and kindness are highly appreciated and will not be forgotten. Esports is a social and positive phenomenon – you are the proof of that!

Anne Fis

Photo credit Emily Mudie Photogra

Johnny Troset Ander

Photo credit Frang

AUTHOR BIOGRAPHIES

ANNE FISH

Based in Surrey, UK, Anne has acted as her son Benjy "benjyfishy" Fish's manager since he signed with the esports organisation NRG, in March 2019. She has been involved in all the logistical and practical aspects of Benjy's career, such as arranging all travel, accommodation and tournament schedules as well as external negotiations and legal matters. Through her role as an esports manager, she has gained a unique insight and extensive knowledge about the competitive world of Fortnite and esports. Anne is passionate about supporting parents of new professional players as an esports mentor and helping to guide the next generation of aspiring professional players, and is an advisor for the Coalition of Parents in Esports (COPE). Anne connects with Fortnite fans through her social media under the alias mamabenjyfishy. In 2021, Anne started playing Fortnite herself and became the first-ever mum of a professional gamer to sign for an esports organisation, Galaxy Racer Esports (GXR).

JOHNNY TROSET ANDERSEN

Johnny lives in Oslo, Norway with his wife Solfrid and two sons, Mikael and Martin. He has worked in the technology industry for three decades and co-founded Genus (www.genus.no), a low-code software company where he holds the position of Chief Technology Officer (CTO). Johnny discovered the esports industry when his youngest son, Martin "MrSavage" Foss Andersen, placed second in the European Fortnite Winter Royale Qualifiers in 2018. Johnny has built a team of esports experts such as managers, agents and legal support around his son, and he helped Martin join the esports organisations NRG in 2019 and 100 Thieves in 2020. Johnny continues to oversee his son's business operations, and is committed to sharing his knowledge and experience through his website www.deeperdown.com, featuring articles and blogs which explore topics surrounding the esports and tech industries. He is an advisor for the Coalition of Parents in Esports (COPE). Johnny is on Twitter under the alias MrTroset.

GLOSSARY

100 Thieves – A lifestyle, gaming and esports organisation based in Los Angeles, California. Often abbreviated to "100T".

200IQ – In gaming, this is an informal reference to a player's high intelligence, strategy and analytical skills. Martin earned a reputation among his fans as having a 200IQ early in his career and subsequently changed his Support-A-Creator Code (see page 210) from "MrSavageM" to "200IQ".

AdvanceClass – Esports educational videos for improving gameplay published by AdvanceClub.

AdvanceClub – A Silicon Valley company providing educational videos and gameplay updates for a monthly subscription fee.

AS, BR, ME, NAE, NAW, OCE – Abbreviations for Fortnite regions (see **Regions**).

Battle Royale – An online multiplayer last-man-standing gaming genre. Fortnite has multiple game modes, with "Fortnite Battle Royale" being the competitive esports mode. Within the competitive Fortnite Battle Royale community, the term "Fortnite" refers to the Battle Royale game mode.

Bootcamp – Players coming together at a physical location to practise their gameplay, play competitively as solo players and as a team, as well as socialising together. Bootcamps often take place before larger LAN events (see **LAN**).

BYOC – Bring Your Own Computer - A LAN event where you bring your own PC, monitor and peripherals. At larger BYOC events it is often possible to rent equipment.

Cash cup – Online tournaments within Fortnite Battle Royale where top placing players receive cash prizes. This is opposed to tournaments where top prizes are things like cosmetic items (skins in Fortnite) or clout (mentions on social media).

ClubNow – AdvanceClub's video series with monthly updates from their instructors.

Content creator – Someone who creates appealing videos, whether it is live, or edited and then published. In a broader sense this is someone who creates and publishes a variety of audio, video, photographic and written content.

Content Castle – The name of NRG Esports' space in Los Angeles containing a variety of rooms and installations to use for their content creators, influencers and esports players, like a "rage room" stylised as the Oval Office.

Content house – (see **Team house**).

Console – Device made specifically for gaming as opposed to more general-purpose devices like smartphones and personal computers.

Cooler Esports – A European esports organisation with headquarters in London, UK. Cooler closed their operations in April 2021 due to financial reasons.

Drop spot or landing spot – The location where a player lands at the start of a Fortnite Battle Royale game. Some locations are more favourable than others, offering a higher chance of loot. Popular drop spots can be contested by other players, and the selection and practice of landings are an essential element of the Fortnite "early game".

Early game – The first part of a game, which in Fortnite Battle Royale corresponds to a player's landing, building up material, finding loot and fighting off any contestant on their drop spot.

End game or Late game – In Fortnite Battle Royale this refers to the last few minutes of the game, and more specifically the time from around the fifth zone (storm circle) until the game is finished.

Epic Games, Inc – The company that develops and publishes Fortnite.

Facecam – Short for "face camera", i.e. a video camera focusing on your face.

FaZe Clan – An esports and entertainment organisation with headquarters in Los Angeles, United States.

Flank – Attacking an enemy from one or more sides.

Fnatic – A European esports organisation with headquarters in London, UK.

FNCS – An abbreviation of Fortnite Champion Series, an online tournament series organised by Epic Games.

Graphic card – A computer hardware component providing high performance video to monitor screens.

Griefing – Playing with intent to disrupt another player or team in-game rather than playing for one's own best interest.

Grinding – Performing repetitive tasks, like playing many games in Fortnite Battle Royale to gain experience points (XP) and advance in levels. Grinding in Fortnite often means the same as practising.

Hearing loss – A person has hearing loss if not able to hear low whispering or leaves rustling, which corresponds to a measurement of about 20 dB according to the World Health Organisation (WHO).

Influencer – An individual with enough followers or engagement on digital channels like Instagram, Twitter etc. to be able to inspire or guide the attention and actions of others.

IRL – An abbreviation of the term "in real life", as opposed to being online.

Keybinds – The association of a key on a keyboard or mouse to a function in your game, like W, A, S and D for moving your in-game character up, left, down and right.

LAN – A "LAN event", "LAN tournament", "LAN party" or simply "LAN" is a gathering of players at the same physical location where a Local Area Network (LAN) is used to connect the gaming devices, as opposed to connecting over the internet.

Lag or laggy – Slower response than expected from your game, computer or network.

Late game – (See **End game**)

Loot – Objects in Fortnite Battle Royale like ammunition, weapons and shield potions.

Mechanical skills – Skills related to the ability to quickly and precisely control devices like keyboard and mouse. These are physical skills in contrast to other types such as game sense, awareness and positioning.

Mechs – Two-player robots present in Fortnite season 10 ("Season X", August to October 2019). The robots acted like a vehicle, with one player controlling movement and the other weapons.

Meta – Literally means "about" or "beyond", and in gaming translates to information about the game and the most effective tactics available based on the current items and rules in the game.

Mid game – In Fortnite Battle Royale this corresponds to the part of the game between surviving and leaving the drop spot and the late game.

MMB – An abbreviation of the popular Fortnite trio consisting of the players Mongraal, Mitr0 and benjyfishy.

Mod – An abbreviation of moderator. In streaming this is someone that ensures that the stream chat meets content standards by removing offensive posts and spam.

Motherboard – The main hardware component of computers containing parts like the central processing unit (CPU), random-access memory (RAM) and connectors for peripheral devices.

NA – An abbreviation of North America.

NGL – An abbreviation of the phrase "not going to lie".

NRG – A professional esports organisation based in Los Angeles, California, United States. "NRG" is to be pronounced "eNeRGy".

Org – An abbreviation for esports organisation.

Over the top content – Content going beyond what is expected, like a short video film with an unexpected and fun ending.

Pro-am – An event involving both professionals ("pro") and amateurs ("am").

Regions or Fortnite regions – The Fortnite regions include Asia (AS), Brazil (BR), Europe (EU), Middle East (ME), North America East (NAE), North America West (NAW) and Oceania (OCE).

ROCCAT – A German brand and computer peripherals manufacturer bought by Turtle Beach Corporation in 2019.

Rotate or rotations – Moving between points of interest on the map in-game. Good rotations in Fortnite Battle Royale typically involves tactical elements like avoiding (or engaging) enemy players, gathering as much loot and material as possible and ending up in a good position for the late game.

Scrim – Practice games against several players or teams. The word is derived from "scrimmage".

SDI – Serial Digital Interface is a standard for digital video transmission over cable for broadcast-grade video.

Shoutcasting – Live commenting of games to entertain and inform the viewers.

Sniping – In Fortnite this is to shoot another player accurately at a long range with a rifle, typically from a place where the shooter cannot be seen by the other player.

Solary – An esports organisation based in Tours, France.

STEM – Short for Science, Technology Engineering and Mathematics.

Streamer – A person broadcasting live on an online platform like Twitch or YouTube Live. Examples of stream categories on Twitch are "Just Chatting", "Valorant" (a video game), "Travel & Outdoors" with "Fortnite" being one of the largest.

Streamlabs – A company delivering software for live broadcasting and streaming. The software is named "Streamlabs OBS" (where OBS is an abbreviation for Open Broadcaster Software).

Squad – A team in Fortnite Battle Royale consisting of four players (see **Team modes**).

Turbo building – A feature in Fortnite allowing players to build and place structures repeatedly while holding down a button rather than rapidly clicking.

Turtle Beach Corporation – A global gaming accessory company with headquarters in San Diego, USA. Owner of the ROCCAT brand.

Team, gaming or content house – An esports organisation's facility for their various player teams and/or employees. An example is the "Cash App Compound", which is 100 Thieves' 15,000 square feet (1400 m^2) headquarters in Los Angeles, United States, with spaces for esports training, streaming, content production and more.

Team modes – In Fortnite Battle Royale, this corresponds to player team sizes, which are solo, duo, trio and squad, consisting of one, two, three and four players, respectively.

Washed – In gaming, this is a derogatory reference to a player not being so skilful, popular or successful in the game as they used to be.

Victory Royale – The last solo, duo, trio or squad team alive in Fortnite Battle Royale during a game.

Vlog – Video log or video blog, i.e. videos about personal experiences and situations. Gaming vlogs typically do not show much gameplay but more of experiences outside of gaming, like what happens behind the scenes during LAN events or competitions.

VOD reviews – Analysing a game based on replaying game recordings to learn from mistakes and more. Game recordings are named VODs (video-on-demand). The built-in replay system in Fortnite allows for viewing gameplay for any player from any angle.

Zone or safe zone – The zone is the safe area within the eye of the storm inside a Fortnite Battle Royale gameplay. Any player outside the zone takes damage from the storm. The zone is circular and shrinks and moves during gameplay.

First published in 2021 by DeeperDown Publishing

By the time of publishing, MrSavage's personal sponsors were:

ROCCAT® (a Turtle Beach® brand), for their keyboards, mice, mousepads and headsets.
ASUS® ROG® (Republic of Gamers®), for their gaming laptops and personal computers (PCs).
Streamlabs® (a Logitech® brand), for their livestreaming software.
KovaaK®, for their Aim Trainer software.
MrSavage has earlier been sponsored by AdvanceClub® for their Fortnite classes.

This book is not sponsored by or endorsed by any trademarks, companies or esports organisations appearing in the book.

All trademarks are the property of their respective owners.
Fortnite® and Fortnite Battle Royale® are the registered trademarks of Epic Games, Inc.

Every effort has been made to contact copyright holders. However, the publisher will be glad to rectify in future editions any inadvertent omissions brought to their attention.

Photo credits

Cover, layout and illustrations by Callum Bowdler.
Cover photos by Emily Mudie Photography, Trygve Espejord and MrSavage.
Photos credited MrSavage are shot by Martin Foss Andersen, Johnny Troset Andersen or Peter Rudi Pettersen. Photos credited benjyfishy are shot by Benjy Fish, Anne Fish or Henry "rockit" Orvis.

ISBN 978-1-7398316-0-8

Also available as an ebook

ISBN 978-1-7398316-1-5

Design by Callum Bowdler
Editing by Gemma Whelan
Project management by whitefox
Printed and bound by Re:View